BEI GRIN MACHT SICH IHR WISSEN BEZAHLT

- Wir veröffentlichen Ihre Hausarbeit, Bachelor- und Masterarbeit

- Ihr eigenes eBook und Buch - weltweit in allen wichtigen Shops

- Verdienen Sie an jedem Verkauf

Jetzt bei www.GRIN.com hochladen und kostenlos publizieren

Bibliografische Information der Deutschen Nationalbibliothek:

Die Deutsche Bibliothek verzeichnet diese Publikation in der Deutschen Nationalbibliografie; detaillierte bibliografische Daten sind im Internet über http://dnb.d-nb.de/ abrufbar.

Dieses Werk sowie alle darin enthaltenen einzelnen Beiträge und Abbildungen sind urheberrechtlich geschützt. Jede Verwertung, die nicht ausdrücklich vom Urheberrechtsschutz zugelassen ist, bedarf der vorherigen Zustimmung des Verlages. Das gilt insbesondere für Vervielfältigungen, Bearbeitungen, Übersetzungen, Mikroverfilmungen, Auswertungen durch Datenbanken und für die Einspeicherung und Verarbeitung in elektronische Systeme. Alle Rechte, auch die des auszugsweisen Nachdrucks, der fotomechanischen Wiedergabe (einschließlich Mikrokopie) sowie der Auswertung durch Datenbanken oder ähnliche Einrichtungen, vorbehalten.

Impressum:

Copyright © 2016 GRIN Verlag, Open Publishing GmbH
Druck und Bindung: Books on Demand GmbH, Norderstedt Germany
ISBN: 9783668343337

Dieses Buch bei GRIN:

http://www.grin.com/de/e-book/344518/green-growth-vs-economic-development-with-pollution-throw-away-society

Markus Reiter

Green growth vs. economic development with pollution. Throw-away society vs. sustainability

The role of the customer in the context of sustainability, consumption and waste reduction

GRIN Verlag

GRIN - Your knowledge has value

Der GRIN Verlag publiziert seit 1998 wissenschaftliche Arbeiten von Studenten, Hochschullehrern und anderen Akademikern als eBook und gedrucktes Buch. Die Verlagswebsite www.grin.com ist die ideale Plattform zur Veröffentlichung von Hausarbeiten, Abschlussarbeiten, wissenschaftlichen Aufsätzen, Dissertationen und Fachbüchern.

Besuchen Sie uns im Internet:

http://www.grin.com/

http://www.facebook.com/grincom

http://www.twitter.com/grin_com

Hochschule für angewandtes Management
Fakultät Betriebswirtschaftslehre
Wintersemester 2015/2016

Studienarbeit

Green growth vs. economic development with pollution
Throw- away society vs. sustainability

Tag der Einreichung: 14.03.2016

Table of Content

List of Abbreviations III

List of Figures IV

1 General Insights in throw-away society and sustainability .... - 1 -

2 Waste of Clothing .... - 3 -

    2.1 What is fair fashion? .... - 3 -

    2.2 Lifecycle of a cotton textile .... - 5 -

    2.3 Responsibility of the fashion industry .... - 6 -

        2.3.1 Ecological .... - 6 -

        2.3.2 Health and ethical .... - 7 -

        2.3.3 The sustainable lifecycle of a cotton textile – a solution .... - 9 -

    2.4 Responsibility of the consumer .... - 10

    2.5 Conclusion – What can be changed .... - 10 -

3 Organic food as a solution for sustainable nutrition .... - 11 -

    3.1 Definition of organic food .... - 13 -

    3.2 Chances and risks of sustainable nutrition and organic food .... - 13 -

    3.3 Consumers' motivation for buying organic food .... - 17 -

    3.4 Recommendations given by BCFN (Barilla Center for food & nutrition) .... - 19 -

    3.5 Conclusion and recommendations .... - 20 -

4 Washing .... - 21 -

    4.1 Detergents – harmful to the environment .... - 24 -

    4.2 Detergents – historical background and legal specifications .... - 24 -

    4.3 Environmental responsibilities of companies .... - 25 -

        4.3.1 Product types .... - 25 -

        4.3.2 Protection of resources .... - 26 -

        4.3.3 Water management .... - 27 -

        4.3.4 Worth from waste .... - 28 -

	4.3.5 Social responsibilities	- 28 -
4.4	Environmental responsibilities of consumers	- 29 -
	4.4.1 Washing at low temperatures but long washing times	- 29 -
	4.4.2 Loading the washing machine right	- 29 -
	4.4.3 Right dosage of detergent	- 30 -
	4.4.4 Labels of environmental friendly products	- 30 -
4.5	Conclusion	- 32 -
5	General insights in waste of clothing, food and e-waste	- 33 -
5.1	Waste of Clothing	- 34 -
	5.1.1 Reasons for disposal	- 35 -
	5.1.2 Ways to reduce waste	- 36 -
5.2	Waste of Food	- 37 -
	5.2.1 Reasons for disposal	- 39 -
	5.2.2 Ways to reduce waste	- 40 -
5.3	Waste of electrical and electronic equipment (WEEE)	- 41 -
	5.3.1 Reasons for disposal	- 42 -
	5.3.2 Ways to reduce waste	- 43 -
6	Limitations	- 44 -
7	Implications and future research	- 44 -

List of Abbreviations

CEFIC	EU Chemical Industry Council
EEE	Electric Equipment and Electronics
EDTA	Ethylendiamintetraacetat
E-waste	Electronic waste
FSC	Food Supply Chain
WBCSD	World Business Council for Sustainable Development
WEEE	Waste of Electrical and Electronic Equipment
WEEE	Waste of Electrical and Electronic Equipment
WRI	World Resource Institute and
WWF	World Wildlife Fund

List of Figures

Figure 1 Triangle of sustainability (Institut Bauen und Umwelt, 2016) .... - 2 -
Figure 2 Lifecycle of a cotton textile (own figure, based on Baier &Frese, 2005, p.2) .... - 5 -
Figure 3 Statutory minimum wage and living wage (Luginbühl & Musiolek, 2014) .... - 8 -
Figure 4 The sustainable lifycycle of a cotton textile (own expanded figure, based on BAier & Frese, 2005, p.2) .... - 9 -
Figure 5 Sectors producing the greenhouse gas emissions of European families, Barilla Center for Food & Nutrition, 2015, p. 81 .... - 12 -
Figure 6 The double pyramid of BCFN, (Barilla Center for Food & Nutrition, 2015, p. 14-15) .... - 19 -
Figure 7 Population in Germany with attitude ‚I prefer using environmentally friendly household cleaners and detergents' (2010 to 2013, in million), (own expanded figure, based on statista 2015) .... - 22 -
Figure 8 Attitude towards buying environmentally friendly products, (own expanded figure, based on statista 2015) .... - 23 -
Figure 9 Production, transport and use phase of detergents, (own expanded figure, based on Wagner 2010, p. 292) .... - 24 -
Figure 10 Eco-labeling - Ecolabel, Der Blaue Engel, sustainable cleaning, Bayerisches Landesamt für Umwelt 2013 .... - 31 -
Figure 11 Life cycle assessment-g CO_2-EQ/wash, (own expanded figure, based on Wagner 2010, p. 280) .... - 31 -
Figure 12 Percentage environment effects in the detergents whole life cycle, Wagner 2010, p. 278 .... - 33 -
Figure 13 Conceptual model of reasons for textile disposal behavior (Morgan et al. 2009, p.193) .... - 36 -
Figure 14 Per capita food losses and waste, at consumption and pre-consumptions stages, in different regions (Gustavsson et al., 2011, p. 5) .... - 38 -
Figure 15 Part of the initial production lost or wasted at different stages of the FSC for fruits and vegetables in different regions (Gustavsson et al. ,2011, p.7) .... - 39 -
Figure 16 Campaign of Intermarché of mishaped fruits and vegetables (Cliff, 2014) .... - 40 -
Figure 17 Loop of the material cycle of WEEE, (Khetriwal et al., 2009, pp. 4–5) .... - 42 -

IV

1 General Insights in throw-away society and sustainability

In his Oscar speech, on the 28th of February 2016, even Leonardo DiCaprio, a famous actor, took the opportunity of speaking in front of many people and focuses on the environmental issue we are facing right now:

> *"Climate change is real, it is happening right now. It is the most urgent threat facing our entire species, and we need to work collectively together and stop procrastinating. We need to support leaders around the world who do not speak for the big polluters, but who speak for all of humanity, for the indigenous people of the world, for the billions and billions of underprivileged people out there who would be most affected by this."*(Griffiths, 2016)

In this few sentences, the actor brings it to the point: climate change is real and everybody can do something. When thinking about pollution, one might think about the "big polluters", as the actors indicates (Griffiths, 2016). And indeed, most of literature focuses on the role of the industry and their impact on climate pollution. But, we cannot deny the fact that also the people, i.e. the customer should do something.

We can see the importance of the customer when looking at the economic formula for the equilibrium level of national income:

$$Y = C + I + G + (X-M)$$

The letter C stands for domestic household consumption of goods and services, I stands for domestic real investment, G for government spendings on goods and services and (X-M) stands for exports minus imports of goods and services. This formular represents the aggregate demand function. As we can see in this formular, consumption plays a crucial role in economy (Pettinger, 31.January 2008).

Another part of facing climate change is to focus on the aspect of sustainability. Figure 1 shows the triangle of sustainability. Sustainability affects economic, environmental and socio-cultural issues.

In this theses we would like to combine sustainability and the consumer side of view.
The goal of our paper is to analyze the different areas, where goods are consumed and how waste can be reduced in this areas. This paper will focus on the role of the customer in the context of sustainability, consumption and waste reduction.

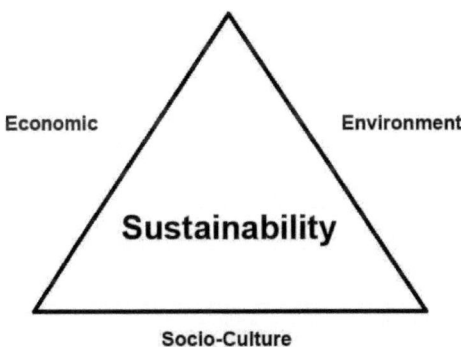

Figure 1 Triangle of sustainability (Institut Bauen und Umwelt, 2016)

We start with the theoretical consideration how clothing /garmin is consumed by the customer. Then we want to shift the focus on different forms of food. Food can contribute to green growth and growth with pollution on both sides. In this section we want to outline the relationship between organic food and sustainable nutrition. Which way of nutrition and consumers' behavior is important for enhancing global sustainability? Furthermore, these questions are viewed by aspects that influence with consumers' behavior, for example the role of the economy, socio-economic factors and the environment. After talking about these external factors, we are having a closer look concerning the internal consumer orientated factors, called motivation. What drives the consumer to buy certain food or not? At the end of this chapter there is an individual recommendation for consumers.

In the next part, we pay attention to washing/ detergents and their impact on sustainability. In the last chapter of our thesis, the topic waste will be explained and the mechanism in the three areas clothing, food and washing to reduce the waste made by the consumer will be presented. In the end, we present our findings and evaluate these results to provide recommendations and derive implications for the future research.

2 Waste of Clothing

Clothing and fashion are present topics in every household. There is a rising demand of fashion because of several reasons. One reason for this demand are the more frequent changing fashion lines. A second reason is the development of the psychological marketing, trying to promote customer impulses for buying fashion. This is complemented by a lot of people who name shopping as a favorite leisure activity and the last reason is the low prices. (Jackson, 2014)

These are a lot of reasons, caused by every single household, that need to be changed.

The explained demand increases the waste of clothing, for example an average U.S. citizen trashes about 32 kilogram of clothing every year and the kilogram of discarding in other first world countries is a quite similar number. (Jackson, 2014).

This behavior is going to cause in the one side ecological problems and on the other side ethical ones. 17 to 20 % of the industrial water pollution is caused by the fashion industry. A result of dyeing and treatment and the usage of about 8000 different chemicals which are used to generate fashion out it raw materials.. Additionally 2.6% of the global water demand is caused by the cotton which is used to create textile. This water demand and pollution will lead to an exceed of the supply to the demand of water by 40 % by 2030. (Jackson, 2014).

An also important aspect of this are the poor conditions for workers in the textile industry, regarding safety, health and ethical aspects. (Muthu, 2015, p. 272)

Regarding this facts about the current situation some basic questions come up which will be clarified in the following chapters, based on the main issue how to act sustainable. What about fair fashion, what is it and what is the outcome? Furthermore, what are the responsibilities of the fashion industry and what are those of the consumer? For this the insights of the fashion industry should be clear, how does cotton become a white shirt and what impacts on the environment and the society does the measurement mean? In the end all this questions should be clear.

2.1 What is fair fashion?

Several labels and signs stand for fair fashion, sustainable fashion, eco labels and a lot of other terms, which can be seen in the following definitions. There is need to clarify how this ethical, fair and sustainable fashion is defined.

One Standard definition is given by the International Standards Organization (ISO), they define eco-fashion as "identifying the general environmental performance of a product within a product group based on its whole life-cycle in order to contribute to improvements in key environmental measures and to support sustainable consumption patterns." (Claudio, 2007).

Sustainable is defined as "involving the use of natural products and energy in a way that does not harm the environment" and "that can continue or be continued for a long time". (Oxford University Press, 2005, p. 1548). According to a cutout of the full definition, fair is "acceptable and appropriate in a particular situation" and "treating people equally – treating everyone equally and according to the rules or law". (Oxford University Press, 2005, p.548). And also the word ethical fits logically in this definitions: "1 connected in beliefs and principles about what is right and wrong [...] 2 morally correct or acceptable". (Oxford University Press, 2005, p. 520).

Based on this a lot of labels can be found, that name themselves in one of this ways, and also a lot of seals, which sign labels as fair, ethical or sustainable. A short overview of important aspects of some popular seals is following.

GOTS: (Global Organic Textile Standard International Working Group, 2014)

- more than 70 % of fibers of controlled biological cultivation
- 10% synthetic fibers are allowed in socks and leggings and 25% in sportswear
- no use of genetic manipulated seeds
- no use of harmful chemicals
- save and ethical working conditions (including working time)
- minimum wage
- offering a regular employment

FAIR WEAR: (Fair Wear Foundation, 2009)

- save and healthy working conditions (including working time)
- living wage
- legally binding employment contracts
- regular supplier controls

FAIRTRADE CERTIFIED COTTON: (Christliche Initiative Romero, 2012, p. 40 f.)

- fairtrade - bonus
- no use of genetic manipulated seeds

- minimum wage guarantee
- locally education and advice
- save and ethical working conditions

2.2 Lifecycle of a cotton textile

To understand the insights of the fashion industry the lifecycle of a white shirt will be explained in the following chapter. Because of globalization it is possible to wear clothes, produced and grown in several different countries, in nearly every country of the world. Globalization is also responsible for the lowest prices beside the widest spread. (Claudio, 2007).Also cotton produces waste, all the pesticides used to strengthen the plants and guarantee a high production rate to conduct a bigger harvest cause damages to the environment. (Claudio, 2007).Every single step of this lifecycle, displayed in figure 2 can have various different impacts on humans and the environment.

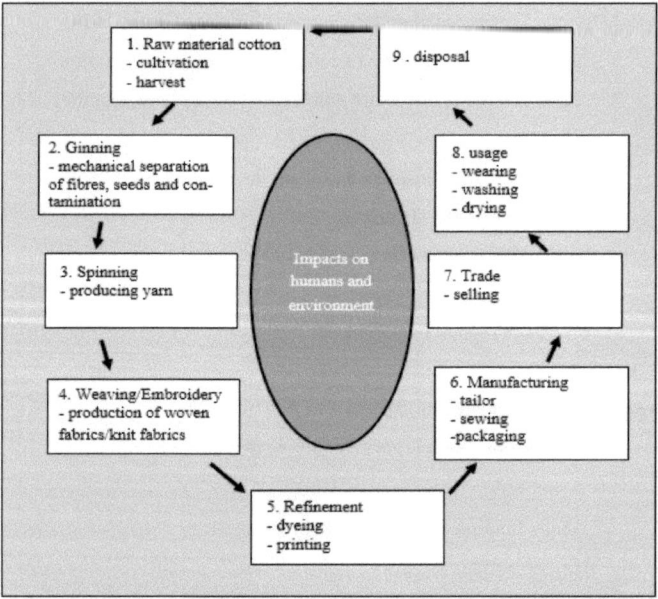

Figure 2 Lifecycle of a cotton textile (own figure, based on Baier &Frese, 2005, p.2)

The responsibilities of the industry and every single consumer are explained in the following chapters.

2.3 Responsibility of the fashion industry

On the one hand there is the fashion industry, which produce and sell clothes and on the other hand there is the consumer, who buys this clothes. So it´s the responsibility of both of them to change the actual situation. The following chapter focuses on the responsibility of the fashion industry, ecological and health and ethical problems are shown, which need a change. Afterwards a solution in the form of a sustainable lifecycle of a cotton textile is displayed.

2.3.1 Ecological

Regarding the enormous resource consumption in the fashion industry also the usage of cotton has risen to 25 million tons in 30 years, this means also the cotton fields have grown. (Environmental Justice Foundation, 2007, p.3)
There is a lot of more different sorts of fiber used than cotton, for example polyester. Polyester is a synthetic material made out of petroleum and is the most manufactured fiber. Synthetic materials cause an energy intensive process and emission of acid gases, for example hydrogen chloride, and of volatile organic compounds completed by a big amount of crude oil, when manufacturing with them. This explained problems are going to raise because of the demand of polyester is nearly doubled in the last 15 years. (Breyer, 2012). That means polyester is now the most used fiber. (Fletcher, 2008, p. 6)
From 1960 to 2000" the Aral Sea lost approximately 70% of its volume as a result of diverting water to grow cotton in the desert." Caused by over 53% of the global cotton fields that need watering because of regional water shortage. (Jackson, 2014)
Each ton of dyed fabric needs 200 tons of water in a single mill in China, this colours reappear in many rivers, which are intoxicated by the dyes wash off from the mills. "As of February 20th, 2012, the China Pollution Map Database had 6,000 records of textile factories violating environmental regulations, including: discharging wastewater from hidden pipes; discharging untreated pollutants; improper use of wastewater treatment facilities; exceeding total pollutant discharge allowed; and using production facilities that were shut down by the authorities for various reasons." (Breyer, 2012). Also in India, in the region Tirupur, most of the 750 factories which dye and bleach run their waste water without cleansing into the nearby river Noyyal. (Starmanns, 2010, p. 26 ff.).
Additionally in Brasil twelve different pesticides can be proved in the rainwater, these pesticides are used on the regional cotton fields. (Environmental Justice Foundation, 2007, p.3)

Cultivating mono cultures and the usage of pesticides and fertilizers lead to a lot of negative impacts in an ecological way. Among others this impacts are serious health problems, less soil fertility, loss of bio diversity, pollution of water, air and ground and a higher resistance of insects and more parasites. (Environmental Justice Foundation, 2007, p. 3; Fletcher, 2008, p. 8 f.). Studies show, that this pesticides, used to cultivate cotton, may be evidenced later in the clothing. (Environmental Justice Foundation, 2007, p. 3).

2.3.2 Health and ethical

Cotton is cultivated in the USA, after the harvest the cotton is sent to China because of their low production prices. There the fashion is made. China is the largest exporter with 30 % of full exporting in clothing sector. The workers have poor conditions, they work for 12-18 cents per hour in the fashion sector. That´s why China is able to have lowest prices in the world competition, by paying nearly no wage and the production costs are at the minimum according to figures of the U.S. National Labor Committee and the UN Commodity Trade Statistics database. (Claudio, 2007).

Synthetic materials, like polyester, and their by-products can cause respiratory disease. (Claudio, 2007).

Supplemented by the pesticides, which are used on the cotton fields, which contaminate the rivers and mean health impairment for the workers. (Environmental Justice Foundation, 2007, p.3). For example in Uzbekistan pesticides were used, which are that toxic that they were prohibited in the Soviet Union, because of intoxicating the air and the floor. (Environmental Justice Foundation, 2007, p.3).

For dyeing, bleaching, tanning and marking textiles chemicals are used. (Baier&Frese, 2005, P.2). Explicitly this chemicals are nonylphenolethoxylates (NPE) and other alkylphenolethoxylates (APEO) as well as additional dangerous substances. Among others they are able to damage the endocrine system. (Greenpeace, 2012, p. 7 f.). NPEs are often used in the textile sector. Greenpeace bought 141 clothes in 29 different countries and found NPE in 63 % of them. (Greenpeace, 2012, p. 3). Furthermore in four clothes they found concentrations of harmful Phtalates and two of them contained cancer-causing amines. Because of this chemicals are washed out of the clothes by normal washing, this chemicals can also be found in german waters. (Greenpeace, 2012, p.7). Moreover the fashion industry uses formaldehydes, which can cause contact allergies and substances to prevent fungal infestations while transporting, they can reduce fertility and attack the nervous system. Because of this reasons they are prohibited in the EU, but they are imported from the non EU manufactures. (Lexikon der Nachhaltigkeit, 2014).

For reasons of cost a lot of production of the fashion industry has been outsourced to third world countries. That´s why new workplaces were created in this countries. (Starmanns, 2010, p. 26). in contrast to this, in Germany the workplaces declined from half a million in 1990 to 167000 in 2002. (Haas & Zademach, 2010, p. 31).

Cotton cultivation is subsidized in the USA since years. Because of this it is possible to have a good quality which is cheap. This fact is also criticized to impact the prices on the global market and by this farmers in other countries are no longer able to competed the cheap prices. (Allwood et al, 2006, p.58). the World Trade Organization (WTO) already exerted pressure on the USA to minimize their subsidies, the USA agreed but still subsidize. According to estimates the global market price would raise about 12.9 %, if there would no longer be subsidies from the US. (Barry, 2006, p.11)

In contrast to this are the subsidies and import duties minimized in India. As a result Indian farmers need to competed with the subsidies of the USA and the thereby accrued global market prices. (Schmitt, 2006).

Wages in the textile industry are very low. While the revenue and profit is rising in this branch the wages of the workers lower. (McMullen & Maher, 2011, p. 1). In august 2013 the monthly minimum wage in the fashion industry was 29 € in Bangladesh (ILO, 2013, p. 2). This is raised in 2013 to 50 €, still not enough to cover the living expenses. (Luginbühl&Musiolek, 2014).

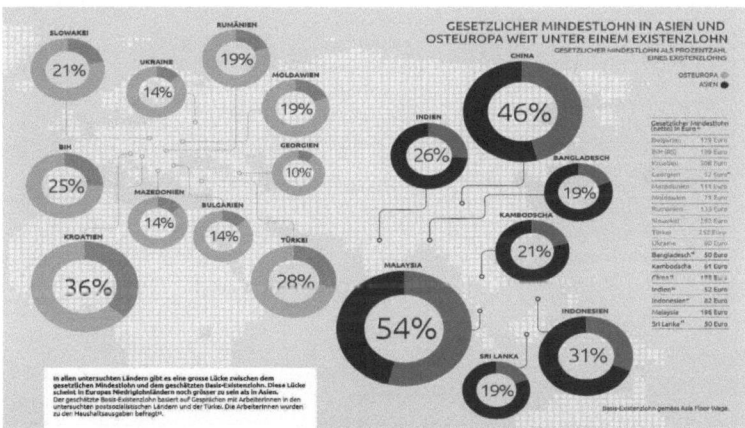

Figure 3 Statutory minimum wage and living wage (Luginbühl & Musiolek, 2014)

The above figure shows the percentage living wage, in different countries in East Europe and Asia, measured on the statutory minimum wage workers receive in the fashion industry. Coming to the point, the part of the minimum wage measured on the living wage is under 50% in every country, except of Malaysia.

Another important point regarding ethical aspects in the fashion industry are working hours. In countries in Asia (like Bangladesh, Sri Lanka, India, Kambodscha, Indonasia, China and Malaysia) twelve hours without lunch break are normal working hours. As a result the employees work for 70 hours and six days per week. (Knieli, 2009, p. 25).

2.3.3 The sustainable lifecycle of a cotton textile – a solution

As a solution, to change all this impacts and problems, the fashion industry should act more sustainable. On the one hand it is possible to act like explained in chapter 2.1. In addition figure 4 - The sustainable lifecycle of a cotton textile also shows a solution – a "green" way – for acting more environmental-friendly, fair and sustainable, based on the already explained improvements.

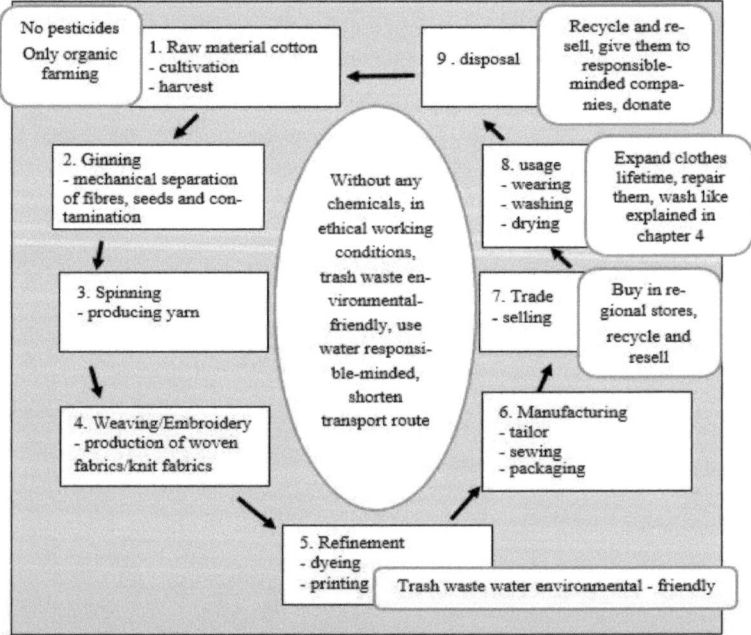

Figure 4 The sustainable lifycycle of a cotton textile (own expanded figure, based on BAier & Frese, 2005, p.2)

2.4 Responsibility of the consumer

Subsequent to the responsibilities of the fashion industry, also the consumer is able to make a change, regarding the named problems, by changing his behaviors. Every consumer is able to have an impact on the manufacturing processes and thereby on the environment and also the social justice with their purchase decisions. (Environmental Justice Foundation, 2007, p. 3).

- **Expand lifetime**: The in chapter 2 explained reasons for the high demand of the new clothes lead to a reduced lifetime of clothes. It is the responsibility of the consumer to extend the average lifetime, if everyone would extend it by nine months it would be possible to make a reduction of carbon, water and waste footprints by 20-30%. (Jenkin, 2015).

- **Recycle clothes:** Mainly there are three ways clothes can be recycled. The first option is to resell them to another consumer, a second one is to give them to developing countries and the last method is to chemically and mechanically recycle them into raw material, so they can be manufactured to other products. This resell and recycle options have grown, thrift shops and outlets have an increasing sale of about 5 % per year. (Claudio, 2007).

- **Repair clothes**: Due to the low prices for new fashion less people repair their clothes to wear them further on. By repairing old clothes their lifetime can be exceeded on the one hand and also less waste is produced. (Fletcher, 2008, p. 101)

- **Buy labeled fashion**: The in chapter 2.1 described seals help the consumer to buy sustainable and fair fashion. A result of doing this would be a better chance for the environment and many humans, a minimization of usage of chemicals and pesticides and also better working conditions for employees and all above mentioned improvements.

2.5 Conclusion – What can be changed

To sum up it can be said, that ethical and ecological aspects have a complex correlation in the fashion industry. In all parts of the lifecycle of a cotton textile negative impacts on humans and the environment can be found. Starting with the manufacturing process which includes a high consumption of raw material and the usage of toxic chemicals and pesticides, which are a danger for health and nature. In the following processes bad working conditions are a current issue, like wages are much under the minimum living wage. Fashion, manufactured under these conditions, is becoming a disposable product because of fashion reasons and cheap prices.

A change of daily behaviors is required to create sustainable fashion consumption as a part of sustainable development. All explained measures, solutions and improvement suggestions have to be seen as a step to a more sustainable handling. The first decisions have to be made at the step raw material cultivation in the lifecycle of a textile. Fibers, which cause minimal influence on human and environment while cultivating should be selected. In no step of the lifecycle harmful chemicals should be used and working conditions have to be ethical and fair. Textile siegnets can help the consumer to get to know the details of the manufacturing of the clothes. Additionally they should always remember, the fewer clothes they consume, the more sustainable is it. That´s a reason to treat the clothes right to expand the lifetime, for example small ruptures can be repaired. Also the improvement suggestions in the following chapter washing help to reduce waste of energy in correlation to the lifecycle of textiles. After the lifetime of a textile it is important to support a sustainable circulation in the fashion industry by recycling.

3 Organic food as a solution for sustainable nutrition

First of all, talking about an industry means talking about facts and growth rates. In the US the annual personal income was 35,985 Dollars per capita and 9.5 % of this total amount was spent on food expenditures in 2009 (Schnepf & Richardson, 2011, p. 7).

In order to capture the dimension of the organic market, it is believed "that organic sales have increased by nearly 20% annually since 1990, with consumer sales reaching $13.8 billion in 2005" (Winter & Davis, 2006, p. 117). Nevertheless, organic agriculture is just a small part of the whole global agriculture industry and its influence in global issues and interests, for example in international trade, is of course limited (Kristiansen, Taji & Reganold, 2006, p. 2).

Nowadays organic food suppliers and retailers merge in a very complex system with a lot of different sectors working together and depending on each other. The European Commission of Agriculture and Rural Development points out that in 2010 there were 186.000 organic farms in Europe. Italy is the pioneer during the observed four last years followed by Spain, France, Germany, Austria and Poland (Eurostat FFS Data, 2015, p.17).

According to a study it is remarked that the majority of the respondents is in favor of organically grown food due to the fact that in conventional food is an uncertain amount of pesticides that is supposed to harm people's health. That is why the question occurs, are these people willing to pay the extra charge for having organic food in the future? (Winter & Davis, 2006, p. 117) What else can be done to reduce the negative environmental effects caused by people's consumption? It is stated that "the consumption of food causes 30% of the emissions of Western families [what] is one of the main causes of climate change" (Barilla Center for Food & Nutrition, 2015, p.80). The investigation shows the environmental burden caused by "greenhouse gas emission, eutrophication, acidification of water and reduction of the atmosphere's ozone layer" (Tucker, 2006).

Figure 5 presents which products have the biggest impact in the environment throughout the whole production chain. Thus there are differences regarding the gas emissions caused by different food. The production chain of meat causes the main percentage of the overall gas-emissions of the food industry.

Where is the starting point to make our economy greener and more sustainable? Kristiansen et al. (2006) dealed with the question whether "organic agriculture [is] the answer to the sustainability problem" (p. 2).

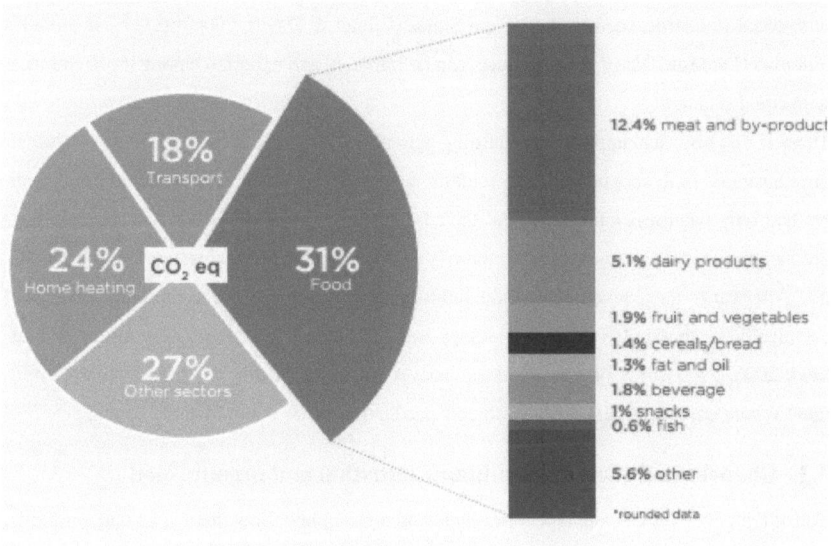

Figure 5 Sectors producing the greenhouse gas emissions of European families, Barilla Center for Food & Nutrition, 2015, p. 81

What steps can be done by the consumer for market growth of the food industry but with less pollution for the environment? How do the three parameters consumer, price and sustainability work well together? The following part will be investigating these questions and revealing the different weak points of this complex system.

3.1 Definition of organic food

Bio-food, also named organically grown food is defined as food "without synthetic pesticides, growth hormones, antibiotics, modern genetic engineering techniques (including genetically modified crops), chemical fertilizers, or sewage sludge" (Winter & David, 2006, p.117). This is what the U.S. regulations demand.

There are also some ways for organic farmers to improve and influence their crop. For example they reuse animal and crop wastes or non-synthetic pest controls. It is important that the fields of organic foods are synthetic and pesticide free for at least three years in order to be sold as bio-food. There is also a similar requirement for animals. They have to be fed nine months with 80% organic nutrition and further three months with 100% organic nutrition. Food enriched with minerals or vitamins are allowed but no antibiotics.

The organic legislation of the EU states that organic products can be imported from countries with equal standards, such as the United States (Winter & David, 2006, pp.117). If these requirements are fulfilled organic products can be imported and exported among those countries with equal standards.

There is one historical approach of defining agriculture by going back to the roots of agricultural business. In the beginning of agriculture there were no chemical interventions and farmers had only natural resources to treat their fields and crops. Due to this fact, organic food production is not a new movement in today's society, it is the original way of the food industry. Afterwards the conventional food industry set in with the break-through research of chemically synthesized fertilizers, biocides and mechanical treatment (Kristiansen & Merfield, 2006, p.4). But is organic food the answer for counteracting the environmental pollution? Where are the limitation of the organic production and is it significantly better?

3.2 Chances and risks of sustainable nutrition and organic food

Considering the chances and risks of organic and non-organic food, there is an odd antithesis. Consumers are supposed to pay the price premium for organic, healthy food that has positive future effects on human's health but on the other hand purchasers of conventional products don't have to pay the "external costs" caused by conventional food, for example negative future impacts on the environment or human health. The positive effects of organic food stays unseen (Workshop on organic agriculture et al, 2003, p.246). This seems to be an unequal contest between those two types of agriculture and their end-products.

But being honest, we have to ask ourselves, if organic agriculture can feed the world? If the answer is no, we have to ask further, are conventional products able to feed the world in a sustainable way? It is said, that this question has nothing to do with the required quantity of food, but with issues like poverty or distribution policies. Studies have revealed that distinctive parameters contribute to a "productive *and* sustainable [organic agriculture]". The market growth of the organic food industry is determined by its society, resource use and the environment (Kristiansen & Merfield, 2006, p.17).

The following chapter focuses on different aspects that play a significant role in sustainable nutrition. Each parameter influences the others. Impacts affecting the consumers are related to health issues, what plays an important role in the consuming process itself, the effects of the food and of course the motivation in people's mind what they decide to eat. Thus, *health* and *socio-economic factors* are also a component. The third component is *economy*. Economic determinants are dominant in the consumers' purchasing power and therefor for the global market industry. In this concept the agricultural yield plays an important role. Even the national policy can intervene by stimulating the agriculture of a country. The last parameter in this complex system is the *environment*. This can be the environment of the country's consumers, for example appearing diseases. But it can also be the economic environment, the force of substitutes or the income amount of consumers. Furthermore, it includes also the environment itself with its nature. If one of these factors is changed the whole system is likely to be changed. A strict separation of these components is not possible.

Economical factor

"Demand is exceeded supply". And the more the demand of people increases the more the prices for those products increases. That's the reason for the premium price categories of organic food. Higher prices relate mainly to products like fruits, vegetable, poultry, eggs and pork than for dairy products (Hallam, p.182).

Researchers remarked that economic yields are equal to those of conventional food (Kristiansen & Merfield, 2006, p.19). Moreover, studies from different universities of the USA demonstrated that over an observation time of 10 to 15 years organically grown crops, like soy beans, wheat, corn and tomatoes had significant harvest in comparison to conventionally grown cultivation. Different regions in the USA showed that organic yields are absolutely comparable to those of non-organic farming. It is also said, that the organic fields are much more heat tolerant (Workshop on organic agriculture, 2003, pp. 39).

But there are also some economic disadvantages regarding the earnings that decrease during the time of change from conventional agriculture to organic agriculture (Kristiansen & Merfield, 2006, p.19). For some farmers this can lead to financial difficulties. Taking the decision to conduct this conversion of their farming is risky and some farmers might be afraid of doing so.

After the conversion to the organic farming system for some farmers the revenue of direct sale is not enough, so they practice a kind of multichannel distribution through direct, indirect/direct by retailers or cooperation with wholesalers. But for the consumer sector the direct contact between farmer and consumer have also positive impact on price. Consumers benefit from the direct contact to the farmer because of the reduced offered price. This is possible because of shorter supply chains. This means less transportation costs and less storage costs and of course less pollution (Canavari & Olson, 2007, pp. 163).

But on the other hand, there are governmental subsidies that enable farmers of non-organic food to produce large quantities of staple food for a minimum price compared to local farmers. That is why some developing countries are able to import these cheap foods and this leads to a competition between the local suppliers and the importing business (Johnston, Fanzo, Cogill, 2014, p. 422).

Environmental factor

On one hand there is the assumption that organic goes hand in hand with ecological sustainability. For example it is certain that soils of organic farms show a higher "biological activity and biodiversity". Furthermore, the negative and harmful impact of pesticides for humans in food is less than in conventional food (Kristiansen & Merfield, 2006, p. 19). Other positive ecological effects of organic agriculture are for example the decrease in polluted water and the improvement of animals' welfare because of the reduction in preventive antibiotic treatment. This aspect has not only to do with the final product itself but also with the daily life of animal husbandry (Workshop on organic agriculture et al., 2003, p. 240). Although it is commonly known that organic production has less negative environmental effects, this way of production and distribution has also its limitations, because the organic agriculture causes also pollution in terms of transportation, waste, storage and other supply chain elements (Johnston et al., 2014, p. 422).

Socio-economic factors

Organic food does no longer mean short distances between farmer/producer and consumer. The organic food industry was also influenced by the globalization process what implies that a growing amount of products are produced somewhere and consumed at the other end of the world. Thus the credibility in organic farming and also products' distribution suffer because of the increasing number of retailers and dealers around the world (Workshop on organic agriculture et al., 2003, p. 240).

Globalization implicates bigger distances the organic products have to overcome what results in negative environmental effects, such as pollution.

To most people organic food implicates that these products are completely produced in their home country. If there is a production chain of several steps it might be difficult to sell the end-product as absolutely organic and contamination-free. That is one reason why organic consumers prefer staple food products, such as eggs, meat, milk, fruit and vegetables from their own country. The import business for fruits, labelled as organic, is therefor quite difficult to conquer (Workshop on organic agriculture et al., 2003, pp. 252).

Considering the consumer side, there is no typical organic food buyer. There is no study that has investigated that there is a demographic relationship between organic consumption and age. Sometimes it seems that more women buy organic food or people who are well-educated. But focusing only one of these isolated parameters is not a successful way of identifying the organic food buyer because it is a quite complex system of motivations (Pearson, Henryks, Jones, 2011, pp.2).

Different groups of consumers might be attracted to different aspects of organic products (Workshop on organic agriculture et al., 2003, p. 240). The concepts has to be adapted to the different kind of groups.

People who are committed to the organic idea/message will always prefer a local farmer's store because this enhances the organic way (Workshop on organic agriculture et al., 2003, p. 242).

On the other hand, there are consumers that prefer the benefits of big supermarkets, where they can get anything they need under one roof. Also these supermarkets have already adapted their portfolio and integrated an assortment of organic food (Pearson et al., 2011, p. 2).

But comparing these two mentioned groups, unfortunately, the fact that people prefer a comfortable way of buying does not go hand in hand with reducing pollution because the organic food in supermarket chains means also storage costs and transportation costs. But to be honest, looking into the future and considering our today's behavior the majority of people will be purchasing in bigger supermarkets, where they can get anything in one purchase instead of going to different stores. That is one point why it is not clear whether organic food sold in single farmer stores is the future answer for sustainability.

After talking about the chances and risks of organic and healthy food, it is also important to have a closer look to conventional food that is still predominant in our daily life.
There are disadvantages of the conventional food that appear not only in the production costs. These are also costs that will be visible in concern of human health, for example long-term damages. Thus for the real cost calculation of conventional food there should be included "medical costs to society of pesticide poisonings and chronic health problems of […] farm workers." Other factors that should be considered while buying conventional food are costs for transportation (non-renewable fossil fuel) or costs for water purification due to pollution from chemical substances. Moreover people also pay indirectly for medical research of antibiotics because animals and humans are already drug-resistant (Workshop on organic agriculture et al., 2003, pp.238).
All in all, it can be said that organic and non-organic food causes sustainability issues and damages the environment to a certain extent.

3.3 Consumers' motivation for buying organic food

The global food market is enormous and that is why organic food and conventional food are direct competitors for consumers. The growing availability of different food makes the consumer more price sensitive. The food market is threatened by forces, for example substitutes. To a certain extent organic food and conventional food are substitutes to some consumers. For some people price plays significant role in their buying decision. Of course consumers with lower income their disposable budget on food is a bigger amount of their total income. So these people are much more affected by price changes or the choice of organic or non-organic purchasing (Schnepf & Richardson, 2011, pp. 1).
Residential food consumption is influenced by several more factors. The advent of diseases such as BSE or contaminated nutrition leads to an increasing awareness towards food consumption. The fear of food related illnesses makes people to buy more expensive food in order to receive healthy untreated nutrition. Therefore it should be examined which points encourage people to buy environment-friendly and organic products. There are two factors that drives the consumers' decision. On one hand the price and on the other hand the health relat-

ed, individual issues. Coming to the point where monetary motivation plays a significant role, called the "willingness-to-pay" a higher price for organic food (Publishing OECD, 2013, p.184). Referring to a survey of the OECD it is stated that people buying organic food because of the individual perception of environmental issues and regulations. The socio-economic or demographic aspect is not a determining factor. But it is not only important what consumers eat, but also how many times a week they eat a certain product, for example meat. The quantity of the consumed food has also environmental impact and influence of consumer food spendings.

Limiting factors are for example the non-constant "trust in the new EU organic food label" (Publishing OECD, 2013, p.185). This leads to the assumption that there is a lack of knowledge about organic food labelling. This hypotheses is also assumed by Lockeritz (2003). He points out that the appearance of undefinable "ecolabels" that refer in some kind to organic products. This development is confusing not only for consumers but also for farmers and regulating authorities (Workshop on organic agriculture et al., 2003, pp. 239). This is a strong disadvantage of organic related products in consumer's mind, because there is no global understanding of what is organic or biological exactly unless you are an expert in this field.

As mentioned above, consuming organic products means different things to different people. Organic food can be regarded as one's way of living and an expression of individual behavior. For others it might be the lower environmental implication or the pesticide-free nutrition itself. One other consumer group is willing to pay the premium because of the better looking and tasting of organic vegetable, fruits or meat. Of course, also organic products do use marketing, so it is a question of individual preference between the brands and advertisings.

3.4 Recommendations given by BCFN (Barilla Center for food & nutrition)

There have been a lot of attempts to give recommendation about a healthier living that is linked to sustainable nutrition. The Barilla Center for Food & Nutrition founded in 2009 gives a short example of how people can easily integrate a sustainable behavior in their daily life, especially in their nutrition. This theory does not take into account whether the products are organic or non-organic. But considering the negative and positive points mentioned above, it seems much more realizable to encourage people to use some of the following guidelines of BCFN than following a certain way of nutrition that is influenced by a lot of different factos. The foundation investigates the close relationship between nutrition and the environment and gives recommendation on how to treat consumers' health and the environment sustainable. All intentions are based on giving information to authorities and consumers. This is also one factor of resolution pointed out in the recent passage.

Figure 6 The double pyramid of BCFN, (Barilla Center for Food & Nutrition, 2015, p. 14-15)

In order to understand the combination of nutrition and environment the foundation created a system called the double pyramid that demonstrates the environmental impact of the consumed food. The following graphic shows the upside down pyramid (right side) of the commonly known food recommendations (left side) next to each other.

The right side pyramid represents the ecological footprint of the different food products, called the "environmental pyramid" (Barilla Center for Food & Nutrition, 2015, p. 11).

The environmental pyramid considers "the impact data as the unit of measurement (per kilogram or liter) for [each] product [category]" (Barilla Center for food & nutrition, 2015, p. 16). The impact consists of three parameters, Carbon Footprint, Water Footprint and the Ecological Footprint. It takes into account the global gas emission and consumption of natural resources. So this is regarded as a guideline for people, who intent living and eating in a healthy way. The result is a positive effect on people's health and by doing so, acting in a sustainable manner. Because of a scientific research it can be remarked that the nutrition, called Mediterranean diet, has less environmental impact than the nutrition of the Americans' today.

By using the dietary guidelines of BCFN, consumers are provided with weekly recommendations of their preferred diet in order to eat healthy and act in a sustainable way.

Summing up, this system also has its limitations because it can't be implemented to every country neither to every culture. Nutrition behaviors are different across the world. Moreover, the pyramid grading of products are too strict and can only be seen also rough guidelines.

3.5 Conclusion and recommendations

To a certain extent it can be estimated that household consumption has major environmental adverse effects on: "food, transportation, waste and water." (OECD Studies on Environmental Policy and Household Behaviour Greening Household Behaviour Overview from the 2011 Survey - Revised edition: Overview from the 2011 Survey - Revised edition 2014, p. 3)

There are some factors that encourage consumers to buy organic products. But these factors have to meet people's demands. This can be for example "price transparency throughout the production process. One other aspect is to raise people's awareness of the external costs that come with the consumption of conventional food, implemented through more advertising for example. These efforts will result in consumers' buying behavior and decision making and they will feel more comfortable when they are better informed about the definition and effects of organic products (Workshop on organic agriculture et al., 2003, p. 247).

As a result of this report, it can be remarked that it seems to be difficult to change the way of producing and distributing food products. Of course, the negative environmental impacts starts with the agriculture but there are limited methods for a resolution. In my opinion it seems rather unrealistic to change the way of agriculture by monetary incentives established by government. The organic or non-organic production is only a part of the whole production chain. At the other end of the production chain there is the consumer. This determining factor is also quite difficult to regulate. Especially in concern of the choice whether to buy organic or non-organic food as they are mostly seen as substitutes with less difference. So in the end, there lasts one point where consumers can be influenced and that is the quantity of each food product they consume. To a certain extent the environmental impact of nutrition is a question of the perfect diet.

What is the consumer supposed to do for a greener environment is the choice of diet for their families. In my opinion for a lot of consumers it is difficult to see the direct positive impact of organic food, also because of some negative headlines and the uncertainty of the inconsistent organic branding.

Looking to the future, there is maybe the possibility to produce tastier meat-free products in order to control the global ecological footprint. Maybe some food can be replaced or substituted by a healthier and more sustainable version or ingredients.

Due to the fact the eating is one of the primary needs of humanity, the discussion of sustainable nutrition and health is certainly an ongoing global issue.

In the following chapter, we would like to shift the focus to washing and detergents and their impact on sustainability and consumption.

4 Washing

The growth rates in household appliance industry show stable development in recent years. In 2013 the industry recognized for the sixth time in a row increasing sales and reported sales of around eight billion Euros. Household appliances are electronic devices, which are used in households as a general rule. These include vacuum cleaner, washing machines, and kitchen appliances like refrigerator, toaster and mixer (Von Siemens bleibt nur das Logo, FAZ.net 2014). In 2012, the worldwide total sales of household appliances reached 176 billion dollars(statista Dossier Haushaltsgeräte 2014, p. 21). Regarding the total sales, the largest companies in the household appliance industry are Haier, Whirlpooland Electrolux.Electronic devices with wide circulation on the german market are especially washing machines and micro waves. In nearly every of the 39 million german households you can find a washing machine (36 million devices) (Statistische Ämter des Bundes und der Länder 2014, online). Combined with the household appliance industry on the one hand, you have the detergent industry on the other hand. The detergent industry is a sub-industry of the chemical industry. The detergent market can be defined as a mature market characterized by Procter & Gamble (Ariel, Febreze, Meister Proper etc.), Unilever (Coral, Domestos, Viss) and Henkel (Persil,

Pril,, Weißer Riese, Somat etc.) as the companies with the highest total sales in this industry. The detergent industry is a very important industry in Germany with 21.000 employees and total industry sales of 7.5 billion Euros. The most important customer countries are France, Belgium, the Netherlands and the UK. The german market of the detergent industry without exports includes a market volume of 4.3 billion Euros (statista Dossier Wasch-, Putz- und Reinigungsmittel 2015, p. 14).

For most of the customers the price is the most important criteria, when it comes to the decision what product should be bought. The brand is just a criteria of only secondary importance. In 2014 a survey showed that more than a quarter of german consumers used Persil in the last three months, which made it to the most favored detergent. A slight majority of consumers is using environmentally friendly detergents (statista Dossier Wasch-, Putz- und Reinigungsmittel 2015, p. 101). An increasing majority of consumers is expressing the wish to offer more mild and considerate detergents as you can see in the figure below.

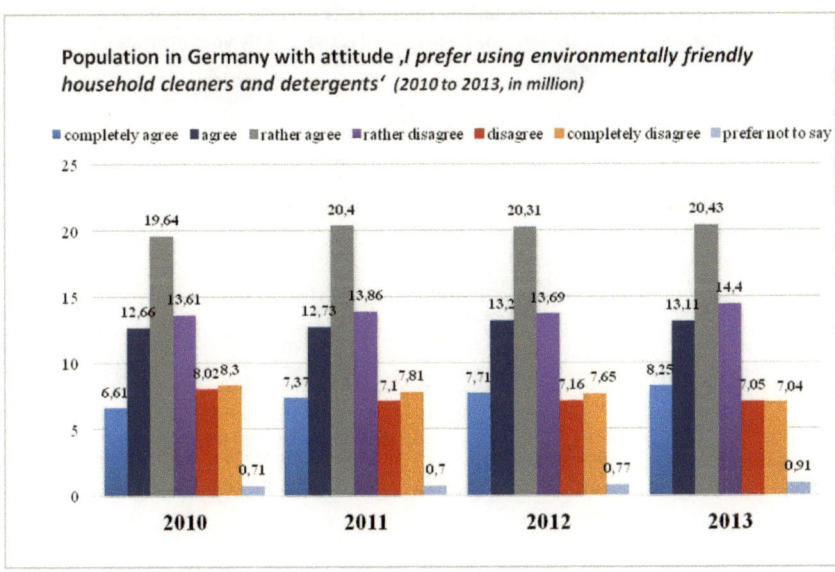

Figure 7 Population in Germany with attitude ‚I prefer using environmentally friendly household cleaners and detergents' (2010 to 2013, in million), (own expanded figure, based on statista 2015)

Because of the injection of harmful chemicals in the water cycle the industry several times was under strong critique in the past. The product development in this industry seems to be quite exhausted. At least the advertising spending in detergents is much higher than the investment in research and development of new products. For example, Procter & Gamble invests around 8.3 billion Dollars in advertising and just 2 billion Dollars in research and development. At Henkel, the advertising importance is even clearer to see. The investment in advertising is ten times higher than investment in product development (statista Dossier Wasch-, Putz- und Reinigungsmittel 2015, p. 89).

In Germany nearly 700.000 tons of detergents are consumed per year which is a consumption of approximately 11 kg per head. With softeners, washing additives and laundry care products the consumption increases to 850.000 tons per year in Germany (Gibt es umweltfreundliche Waschmittel?, Umweltbundesamt 2014). Today a detergent should not only clean the laundry, it also should be environmentally friendly. Many consumers commit to protect the environment and to stop the pollution of the water cycle. But a massive problem is the lack of information, using old habits and the concern over higher costs and effort.

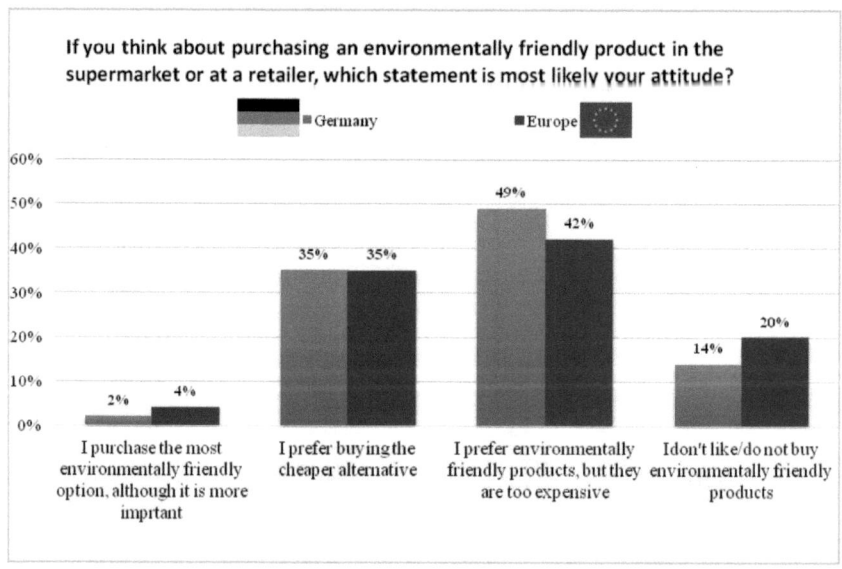

Figure 8 Attitude towards buying environmentally friendly products, (own expanded figure, based on statista 2015)

So an important question is what can be done to get the industry producing more environmentally friendly products and what can be done to convince the consumers of environmentally friendly detergents?

4.1 Detergents – harmful to the environment

All these detergents are made out of chemicals, which get mostly into the wastewater. Because of the heavy usage of detergents, the quantity used and the potential threat is underestimated. Every time using the washing machine, the detergents ingredients release into the wastewater. In 2009, we had an amount of 194.000 tons of tensides, 32.000 tons of phosphates, 8.000 tons of fragrances and 450 tons of optical brighteners in the wastewater (Bayerisches Landesamt für Umwelt 2013, p.3). Many components of detergents are still not easily bio-degradable (e.g. phosphonates, polycarboxylates, EDTA, optical brighteners, fragrances, preservatives). If these chemical substances or their degradation products are not fully filtered or exploited in treatment plant, the chemicals get into the water and water organisms. There, the chemical substances could be concentrated. Also in sludge you can find concentrated components of detergents. If this sludge is used for agricultural land, it will contaminate the farmland and groundwater. Some other components of detergents are this harmful, that these chemicals can affect the consumers' health directly. For example, allergy sufferers react quickly to fragrances and preservatives (Bayerisches Landesamt für Umwelt 2013, p.7).

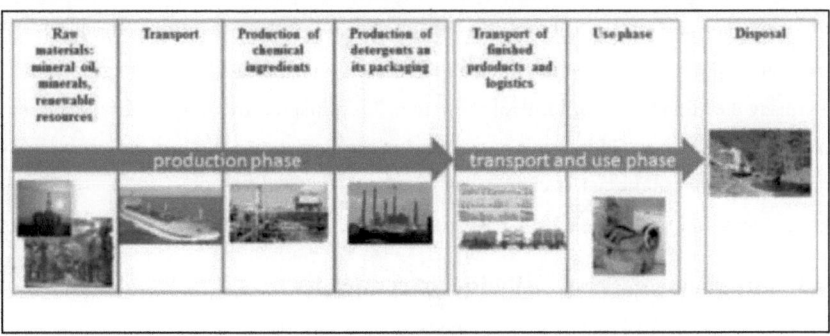

Figure 9 Production, transport and use phase of detergents, (own expanded figure, based on Wagner 2010, p. 292)

4.2 Detergents – historical background and legal specifications

With the increasing usage of washing machines in the middle of the 20th century, the pollution of wastewater and groundwater also increased and there were a lot of foam on the rivers because rivers could not biologically degrade the residual materials of these detergents. In 2005 the European Union placed a new law regarding detergents including softeners and washing agents. Tensides, which are a main component of detergents, must be completely degradable biologically – which means it must be completely degradable from micro organisms to carbon dioxide, water and mineral salts. Complementary to the EU regulation applies the german "Wasch- und Reinigungsmittelgesetz" from 2007. This regulates the criterias regarding the biological attack for specific types of tensides, which are ingredients of detergents, which are not included in the "Detergenzienverordnung". These chemicals mustn't be completely degradable, but only primary biological degradable. With this, they just loose its surface-active characteristics, which means it's not reducing the surface tension of the water. Nevertheless, the intermediates, which it generates could be problematic. For all the other components of detergents the biodegredability is not regulated by law (EG-Detergenzienverordnung Nr. 648/2004, in: Bayerisches Landesamt für Umwelt 2013, p. 2). The producers are obliged to indicate necessarily application notes and precautions on their product packages. For detergents, the producers are although required to put information about the dosage suggestions and the yield on their product packages. Furthermore the companies are committed to list the ingredients: firstly the environmentally relevant substances like tensides, phosphates or optical brighteners, on the other hand preservatives and fragrances, which could be trigger for allergic reactions (e.g. "CITRAL"). More details of the detergents composition must be published on the internet. The reference to the website is also placed on the product packaging. The producers of these products are also obliged to deliver at the request of medical staff for medical purposes a data sheet including all ingredients with indication of its weight share. In Germany the "Bundesinstitut für Risikobewertung" is also a receiver of these data sheets and provides these to the "Giftinformationszentren" of the German states. These centers give advises to parents and doctors, if children get in contact with the detergents chemicals (Bayerisches Landesamt für Umwelt 2013, p.3).

4.3 Environmental responsibilities of companies

On the market you can find an unmanageable number of different detergents. As mentioned before, a main point for consumers on selecting detergents is the environmental friendliness. So the consumer has the expectation to receive products, which fulfill these necessary requirements. In the following is given an overview over product-types, which could help the companies, to fulfill the customers' claims.

4.3.1 Product types

The least environmentally damaging product types are the so called modular systems. Detergent substances, softener and spot remover are just added when required. An alternative is the tandem system. With this system, bleaching agent can be saved. Compared to conventional jumbo- or compact washing powder, ultra- and super compact detergents manage to clean without, for a perfect wash unimportant, excipients and fillers like sodium sulfates. These products just include the, for a perfect wash important chemicals and allow to use a much lower dosage (Wagner 2010, p. 143). So the biological burden of the wastewater and groundwater is also much lower. Furthermore material of packaging and energy consumption are to be spared.

One of the newest developments is the detergent tablet, which is ecologically comparable to the compact washing powder. Liquid detergent includes a very high percentage of tensides. Since 2006 low temperature detergent has been offered, which allows washing with temperatures lower than 30° degrees. There are thus washing machines, offering washing programs with 15° degrees. Newly developed enzymes also remove at these temperatures successfully stains. With its lower power needs the energy-costs are reduced and the emission on greenhouse gases is also reduced. Washing will almost be related with environmental impact because an environmentally friendly detergent is not existing. The main difference is the level of environmentally friendliness (Gibt es umweltfreundliche Waschmittel?, Umweltbundesamt 2014 and Procter & Gamble 2014, Nachhaltigkeitsbericht).

4.3.2 Protection of resources

Regarding ecologically responsibility, there should be the main focus on three core areas.
Protection of resources, renewable resources and worth from waste – value oriented view on production waste. The maxim of conserving resources should be: "more with much less". A main task for the producers is to reduce the quantity of energy, water and materials, which are needed for the production and usage of the detergents, while at the same time the quality of the products should be maintained on a high level (Henning 2006, p. 76). One point to reach the goal "more with much less" is to get the household washing with lower temperatures. This provides the opportunity to reduce the usage of energy and involved greenhouse gas emissions. Recent data indicates that the percentage of wash load in cold wash increases from 2010 until 2014 from 38 percent to 53 percent (Wagner 2010, p. 48). To generate a further growth in using cold wash, the companies are still required to strengthen its consumer information regarding cold wash. The positive results can be measured in Western Europe, where Procter & Gamble implemented campaigns with high visibility (Procter & Gamble 2014, Nachhaltigkeitsbericht).

Another important fact is the cooperation with washing machine manufacturers. With these cooperations the consumers could be informed in three key areas (Procter & Gamble 2014, Nachhaltigkeitsbericht):

1. Placing detergent information about advantages of cold wash on new washing machines. So millions of customers can be reached.
2. Promotion of high speed-wash with saving of time as customer motivation for the election of these washes
3. Development of detergents, which offer the best performance in new energy-saving washing machines.

Another point to reach the goal "more with much less" is to reduce the packaging. Since 2010 the reduction of packaging equals seven percent per packaging unit. More and more usage of efficient products and packaging, less packaging in the logistics chain and usage of new, innovative materials and designs help to reduce packaging materials. Pods in the market of detergents also reduce the packaging material, because the detergent is highly concentrated and takes up only little space. Also in future it is necessary to create products and packaging, which excite consumers on the one hand and on the other hand follow the sustainability target to keep the environmental protection (Wagner 2010, p. 87). This encourages companies, and is a difficult task, to develop additional optimization possibilities. The packaging fulfills an important role, including the protection of the product, the product presentation and the information requirement for the customers. Material and form innovation will be the main task to be developed. The main focus for all the companies producing detergents under ecological criteria shall be an sustainable plan until 2020 with elements like doubling the usage of plastics recyclat in synthetic packaging and the safeguarding, to use packaging with 90 percent reusability respectively establishment of corresponding recycling possibilities (Procter & Gamble 2014, Nachhaltigkeitsbericht).

4.3.3 Water management

Directly connected with the usage of detergents is the usage of water and the ecological responsibility of the companies in water management. The main focus for the producers is divided into two main points:

1. The usage of water, while consumers use detergents
2. The usage of water during manufacturing process.

A life cycle analysis found that the consumer use is the decisive phase during the water consumption. So the ecological responsibility of the producing companies is to develop products with superior performance while washing with less water (Wagner 2010, p. 98). Companies are obliged to force the development of water saving detergents without creating disadvantages for the consumers. Strategic partnerships to fulfill these expectations are inevitable. Partnerships can be formed with institutes and organizations like E4Water, CEFIC (EU Chemical Industry Council), Water Matters, WBCSD (World Business Council for Sustainable Development), WRI (World Resource Institute) and WWF (World Wildlife Fund).

4.3.4 Worth from waste

In the manufacturing process, a lot of different substances and chemicals are used. In order to save the environmental responsibility the waste material should be as little as possible. Also at the end of a products production or life cycle the residual material can be used profitable through reuse, recycling or transformation into energy (Aehle 2007, p.72).

The efforts of reducing waste materials can be diverse. Next to the named solutions the companies can sell parts of its waste material to external partners. These external partners often use these materials for their own manufacturing process.

As an example can be mentioned Procter & Gamble. This company had the innovative idea to reuse absorbable waste material out of their factory in Belleville, Canada. One of their external partners combines their high tech absorbent with other raw material. This results in products which are used for containment and control of leaks (Procter & Gamble 2014, Nachhaltigkeitsbericht).

4.3.5 Social responsibilities

Next to the ecological responsibility, the companies producing detergents also have huge social responsibilities. This includes especially health and hygiene conditions. Responsibilities in the commercial practices are a very important principe for companies in the detergent industry. The interests of the company and every individual are inseparably linked. The companies must be aware of their ethical responsibility, which is linked with the enforcement of laws and respect for every single person. Approaches for this endeavour can be global health-, security- and environment programed. The target is to protect the life, health of the employees and the connected environment and also to protect the factories. The company has to ensure health promoting processes for their employees as well as inhabitants of the surroundings (Becker 2012, p. 14).

It is therefore recommended to enter into a strategic partnership with resources ensure like Health, Safety & Environment (HS&E). This association is responsible for all locations around the world and to make sure that these locations operate safely and legally, manufacturing dangers are minimized or eliminated, health risks get recognized and the factories waste is as much as possible minimized (Wagner 2012, p. 91). With precautions like this, Procter & Gamble for example, was able to minimize their disposed waste quantity and increase the quantity of recycled substances which lead to receipts of 44 million Dollars out of these recycled substances.

Worldwide, there are numerous requirements in the segment of health, security and environment. So the factories have to adhere to the local safety regulations, emission limits and operational requirements (Procter & Gamble 2014, Nachhaltigkeitsbericht).

4.4 Environmental responsibilities of consumers

In the first place for the consumer while using detergents is to have a satisfying result. Next to this the consumer has also to keep in mind his ecological responsibility and a considerate use of resources. This can be reached through changes in the individual detergent usage behavior. In the following different approaches are listed, which help to minimize the usage of detergents. How is it possible to wash sustainable?

4.4.1 Washing at low temperatures but long washing times

Washing machines need a lot of energy to heat up the water, whereas turning the washing drum needs less energy. In accordance with the right detergent a longer washing time will achieve in a better washing result the longer the washing time is. Therefore consumers should use more often lower washing temperatures and longer washing times. This will result in less energy consumption and less detergent usage and furthermore less expenditures (IKW Online 2015 and Bayerisches Landesamt für Umwelt 2013).

4.4.2 Loading the washing machine right

Is a washing machine just half loaded the needed water, energy and detergent isn't halved. A washing machine that is loaded correctly has the advantage to reduce the washing procedure in a 4-member household from 300 to 240 washing procedure per year, which minimized the detergent getting into the waste water and allows the household to save up to 35 Euros per year (IKW Online 2015).

4.4.3 Right dosage of detergent

The average of washing procedures in a 4-member household in Germany is 300. The overdosage of detergents raises the annual consumption immense. How much the dosage should be, can be seen on the packaging. So with reading the recommendation on the packing it's possible to save water and detergent which results in less detergent in the waste water (IKW Online 2015 and Bayerisches Landesamt für Umwelt 2013).

4.4.4 Labels of environmental friendly products

With the quantity of consumed detergent in Germany, the consumers purchase decision can have a strong impact to the market. The easiest way to recognize environmental friendly products is the European eco-labeling "Euroblume" or the "EU Eco-Label". Only this label is awarded through neutral state bodies based on objective scientific criteria. This label has been introduced in 1995 from the European Commission and characterized detergents, which are distinguished by special environmental compatibility and limited health risks. In examinations the whole life cycle is considered – including extraction and processing of raw materials, energy production and packaging (Wagner 2010, p. 99). Therefore in Germany are the "Deutsche Institut für Gütersicherung und Kennzeichnung" and the „Umweltbundesamt" responsible. Furthermore, there are a lot of company labels, but these labels are attached without any public environmental specific inspection of the products. An example for this is the label of the initiative "Initiative Nachhaltiges Waschen und Reinigen" (Sustainable cleaning). This is a voluntarily initiative of the manufacturers of detergents, which are represented in the European association A.I.S.E. (Association Internationale de la Savonnerie, de la Détergence et des Produits d'Entrtien). The association has no minimum requirement for the environmental friendliness of the products, so the label is no official quality mark for environmental friendly products. Participating companies effort to produce and develop sustainable products (Bayerisches Landesamt für Umwelt 2013, p. 13).

Figure 10 Eco-labeling - Ecolabel, Der Blaue Engel, sustainable cleaning, Bayerisches Landesamt für Umwelt 2013

If a consumer is looking for environmentally friendly detergents independently of eco-labels, he can use the following information for orientation:

The detergents yield is an indicator for the concentration strength of the ingredients. Yielding products contain rare fillers and so the environmental impact is less. Concentrates, refill- or returnable packaging systems help to save packaging material. The designation "vollständig biologisch abbaubar" is no seal of quality, this property is required by the law of tensides and softeners and fragrances should not be ingredients of the detergent. Furthermore antibacterial active additives should not be used. Problematic ingredients like phosphates, chlorine, water softener EDTA and NTA, the bleaching agent perborate and brighteners should be avoided (Bayerisches Landesamt für Umwelt 2013, p. 13).

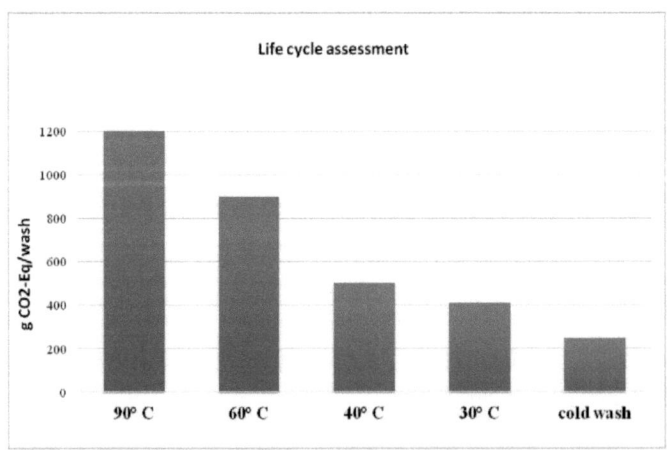

Figure 11 Life cycle assessment-g CO2-EQ/wash, (own expanded figure, based on Wagner 2010, p. 280)

A prominent role is the consumers washing behaviour. All aforementioned improvement possibilities are ineffective, if the consumer doesn't use them in the right way. Like the image above shows, a lower washing temperature goes hand in hand with lower CO^2 emissions. It is for this reason very important to communicate the weak points on the life path of washing. For this reason initiatives like A.I.S.E. got founded to minimize the environmental impact with the right consumer information (Wagner 2010, p. 279).

4.5 Conclusion

Latest since the late 1980's the awareness has been raised, that the population is altering to the global substance flow and the people are changing the global environmental conditions. Causes for this are the strong increase of the world population in the last 50 years, the todays technical possibilities and an energy and resource intensive lifestyle in the industrial countries. To counteract these global challenges a new model is increasingly established: The sustainable growth. A sustainable growth means to meet needs of the current generation without endanger the needs of future generations. It is valid to combine environmental challenges with economic interests and social responsibility (Wagner 2010, p. 284).

A sustainable development always has an economic dimension. That becomes clearer, if you consider the value of laundry. In 2008 in Germany washable textiles were bought with a value of 46.5 billion Euros (Wagner 2010, p. 287). The value preservation is for every consumer of great economic importance and only to ensure through the right washing. Also from the environmental viewpoint, the value preservation is important, because old, unusable textiles are replaced by new ones, which have to be produced with high resource intensive. Next to the industry, especially the consumers are required to be aware of their responsibility while washing. These two players have different assignments in the field of ecology, economics and social issues. The assignments of the detergent manufacturers are to optimize and evaluate ingredients regarding the security of consumers and environment, the responsibility for the products entire life cycles, to offer their products inexpensive, to safeguard jobs, to implement innovations and to offer a simple handling of their detergents. Furthermore they have to minimize the environmental impact by informing the consumers about the right usage, the compliance of legal regulations and reducing the packaging of detergents.

The picture below shows the life cycle assessment and the percentage of the environmental impact of different steps in the detergent life cycle. As you can see especially while using the detergents in the households, the percentage environment impact in terms of energy demand, air pollution and waste is very high.

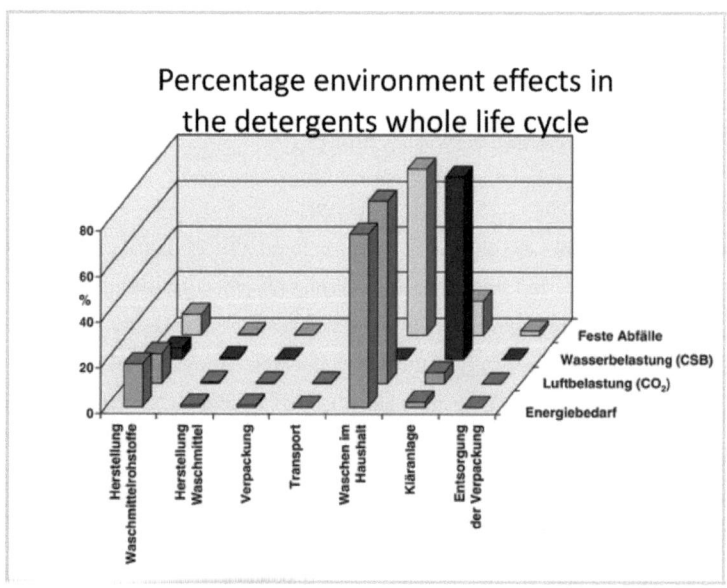

Figure 12 Percentage environment effects in the detergents whole life cycle, Wagner 2010, p. 278

So the assignments of detergent consumers consist out of ecologically, economically and social responsibilities. They have to wash resource-saving, should use low dose detergent, adhere to the packaging advice and right dose of detergent, use the washing temperature as low as possible, have the washing machine fully loaded and do a critical examination of using behaviour regarding the sustainability (Wagner 2010, p. 287). The environmental impact of washing depends to a large extent on doing the right in terms of resource-friendly washing. Even though ecology and economy are no contradiction, because washing right saves money and protects the environment. Because the main environment burdens are caused in the households, it is important to strengthen up the everyday expertise of consumers in this point and provide information and help to use the last years much innovations of detergents and washing preparations in the right way (Wagner 2010, p. 288 and Bayerisches Landesamt für Umwelt 2013 and Umweltbundesamt 2014).

5   General insights in waste of clothing, food and e-waste

In the following chapter, I would like to concentrate on waste. I would like to start to give general insights in waste, then I would like to focus on the aspects food, clothing and washing and give implications of why waste is disposed and how to reduce waste. The following questions will be answered: What is waste? How can waste be reduced in the areas of clothing and washing? What are specific recommendations for customers to reduce food?

We have to be aware of the fact that the three issues described above, clothing, food and washing, automatically go along with waste. Whenever goods, services or products are produced, waste will be generated. Due to the fact that we live in a throw-away society (Ritch, Brennan, & MacLeod, 2009, p. 168), the topic waste has gained more and more attention.

According to Dhalgaard and Dhalgaard (2002), waste is defined as "everything that increases cost without adding value for the customer" (p. 1076). This definition clearly focuses on the role of customers or households, who are at the end of the value-added chain. It is clear that the customers' behavior plays an important role in economic issues and sustainability (Ritch et al., 2009, p. 169).

Other actors in the context of waste are among others governments or companies, i.e. producer. For firms, it is difficult to quantify the amount of waste as a whole. This is due to the fact that waste is never measured or registered as a whole in companies' systems (Dahlgaard & Dahlgaard, 2002, p. 1076).

The political recognition for waste has been growing over the last decades (Ritch et al., 2009, p. 169). One example where the government takes action to reduce waste and therefore the environmental pollution is the ban of plastic bags. Due to its enormous environmental pollution in the oceans (Aldred, 2008), the use of plastic bags has been banned by the local government in several countries (Ritch et al., 2009, p. 170).

Given the emphasis on sustainable growth and development, politics and consumer pay more attention on social and environmental impact of particular methods of production and on particular products. It is crucial to optimize policy regarding linkages between the production and consumption of services, products and goods and adjust them to the principles of sustainable growth and development (Ritch et al., 2009, p. 168-169).

In the next chapters, the focus will be on the role of the costumer in the context of waste.

5.1 Waste of Clothing

The lifecycle of waste can be categorized in three stages: waste produced by manufactures, called "post-producer waste", "pre-consumer waste" which is generated by retailers, and waste generated by the public, which is called" post-consumer waste" (Domina & Koch,

1997, p. 99). The last type of waste indicates that customers play an important role in the context of waste.

Given this fact, they also need to be seen as stakeholders of the productive business (Niinimäki, 2010, p. 161) and as "responsible actors in fashion" (Niinimäki, 2010, p. 152). Since the amount of cheap garment increases, consumers purchase those sometimes even despite their ethical values and interests. It "confuses consumers' rational behavior, preventing them from buying more expensive clothes and investing in better quality and sustainability" (Niinimäki, 2010, p. 161). It is believed that consumer determine the lifespan of apparel, the potential of recycling and reusing clothes and the amount of generated waste of apparel (Laitala, 2014, p. 444).

5.1.1 Reasons for disposal

Due to the fact that materials are often placed with perceived and intrinsic value, consumers prefer to pass clothing to friends and family, donate it (p. 233) or even store it at home (Koch & Domina, 1999, p. 13) rather than throw it away (Laitala, 2014, p. 454). Morgan & Birtwistle (2009) quantify this and indicate that nearly one-quarter of fashion items were given to family members or friends, while a fifth of clothing was reused in the home (p. 195). Indeed, reasons for donating clothing to charities are among others that the donation result in a better feeling by the donor. Another reasons is the belief that unfortunate persons might be able to buy used clothing at lower prices (Bianchi & Birtwistle, 2010, p. 364). It is believed that most consumers are not aware of other ways of recycling, besides reusing or donating. In contrast to this, reasons for disposal are among others poor fit, damages or even lack of storage space (Laitala, 2014, p. 454). As we can see in Figure 11, Morgan & Birtwistle (2009) indicate that even fashion might be one factor which determines textile disposal behavior (p.193).

This is also underlined by the study of Domina & Koch (2002). The authors come to the conclusion that clothing is disposed only because of fashion reasons, this means because it is not fashionable anymore. This happens even though the clothing is not damaged.

However, given the fact that households recycle, significant predictors for recycling clothes are family size, demographics of age as well of income (Domina & Koch, 2002, p. 234)

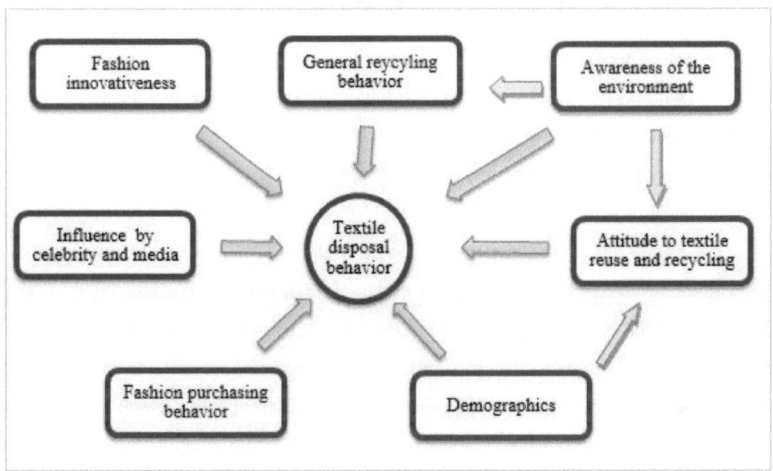

Figure 13 Conceptual model of reasons for textile disposal behavior (Morgan et al. 2009, p.193)

5.1.2 Ways to reduce waste

It is a general belief that education initiatives have strengthen the awareness of waste disposal in the society. Recycling of paper, glass or plastic are now common materials, which get recycled. Customers need to get a broader range of recycling methods for other materials, such as garment, textiles and apparel. Government could offer economic and technical support for entrepreneurs who are dealing with garment waste recycling (Domina & Koch, 1997, p. 101). One option is to collect unneeded garment by curbside textile collection. To guarantee the success of such collection programs, individuals need to be encouraged to understand the effect of textile recycling on the environment as well as one's personal economy (Koch, & Domina, 1999, p. 14).

However, recycling of textile and apparel has great potential of being reused and recycled, unfortunately this potential has not been used yet (Koch & Domina, 1999, p. 4). This is linked to strengthening consumers' awareness of recycling through education programs. Consumers should be educated of the types of textiles products, which can be recycled and the benefits of recycling textiles (Koch & Domina,1999, p. 14).

This is underlined by the study of Morgan & Birtwistle (2009) who capture the role of gender in the context of recycling clothes of households. They come to the conclusion that female customer are unaware of the need of recycling clothes. They often do not know how cotton is produced and what effect recycling clothes has on the environmental consequences. This is resulted by a lack of media coverage. It is believed that media coverage will result in change in behavior by retailers and producers. They have to adapt their sales strategies and collection on the environmental impact of textile waste (p. 196).

Another possibility to consider for decreasing textile waste is to focus on the speed of the clothing industry. Retailers such as Zara or H&M are examples of the fast fashion industry. These companies are launching new lines once or twice per month at very low prices and therefore enhance their sales through impulse purchases (Bianchi & Birtwistle, 2010, p. 353). Slowing down the product lifespan and therefore having a longer lifespan of garment will reduce the waste of energy as well as the consumption of natural resources. It will encourage customers to buy less garment and spend more money on higher quality which is more durable (Jung & Jin, 2014, p. 512). Capturing this in a nutshell: Customer buy higher quality, wear it a longer period of time, wear it more often and in several ways (Jung & Jin, 2014, p. 517). It is shown that the slow fashion is found to be driven by customers who care less about fashion trends and more about the lifespan of the product. They want to wear it in multiple ways. Customer who are interested in slow fashion also are interests in the influence of clothes on producers and on societies (Jung & Jin, 2014, p. 517). As we can see, slow fashion might be a good opportunity to decrease clothing waste on a long-term perspective.

5.2 Waste of Food

Many resources are wasted when food is produced, including energy, water, land and the economic value of the product. Products, respectively food, which is not consumed lead to Co2 Emissions which could have been saved (Gustavsson, Food and Agriculture Organization of the United Nations, & ASME/ Pacific Rim Technical Conference and Exhibition on Integration and Packaging of MEMS, 2011, p. 1).

As we can see in Figure 14 there are country specific differences in the amount of how much waste consumers and production to retailing generate. In General, between 30 and 50% of produced food is not consumed, respectively not eaten by humans (Ridoutt et al., 2014, p.

6107). Globally, one third of the edible party of food is wasted. This represents about 1.3 billion ton per year which are wasted (Gustavsson et al., 2011, p. 4). In fact, food gets lost along all stages of the food supply chain (FSC) (Koivupuro et al., 2012, p. 184), including (agricultural) production of food (Gustavsson et al., 2011, p. 4), retailing and those stages which participate in food storage, purchase and preparation like households (Ridoutt et al., 2014, p. 6107). Some examples of waste along the FSC are: spilling during harvest operation like fruit picking (agricultural production), crops which are sorted out during washing or peeling (processing) or waste in market systems (distribution) (Gustavsson et al., 2011, p. 2).

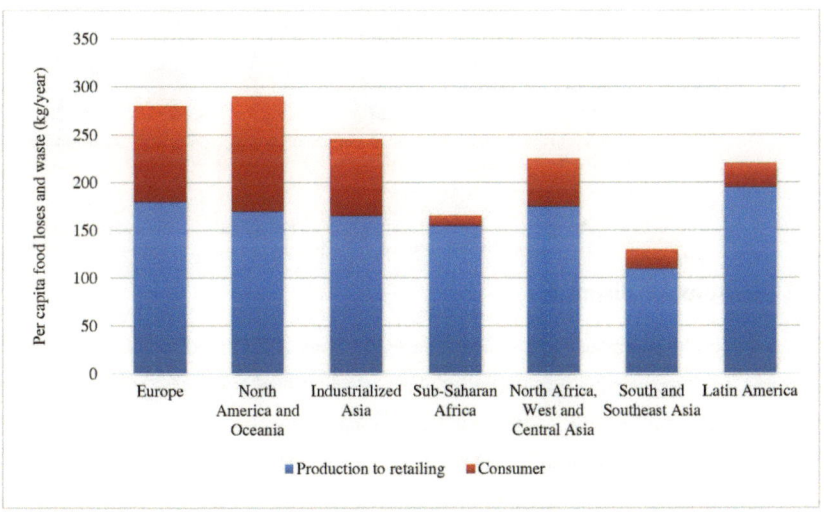

Figure 14 Per capita food losses and waste, at consumption and pre-consumptions stages, in different regions (Gustavsson et al., 2011, p. 5)

Figure 15 shows the distribution of waste generated on each stage of the FSC by fruits and vegetables. It shows that there are considerable differences on the volume of processing-waste. The amount of food of the different stages wasted in the single stages of the FSC depend on the fact whether countries are developing or industrialized ones. In developing countries more than 40% of food waste occurs in processing levels or post-harvest. In industrialized countries more than 40% of food is wasted at the retail or consumer stage. The amount of food waste is quite the same on both types of countries (Gustavsson et al., 2011, p. 5).

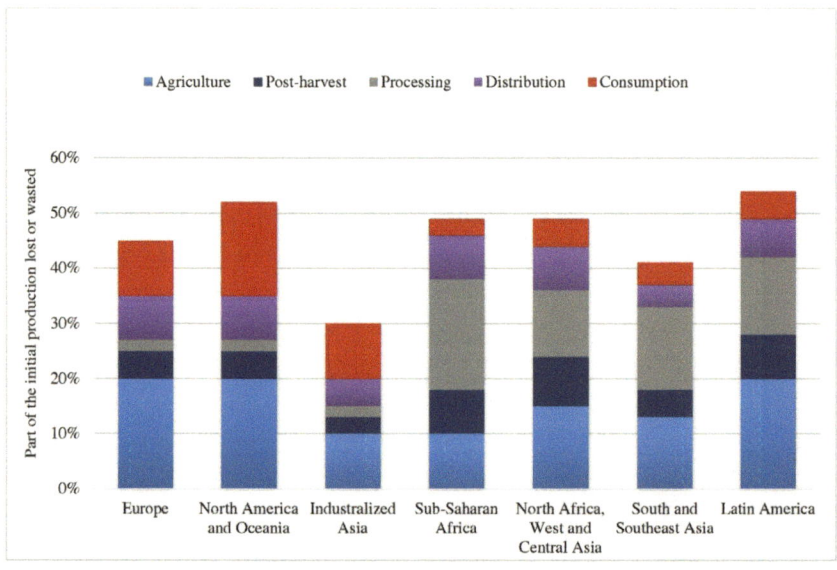

Figure 15 Part of the initial production lost or wasted at different stages of the FSC for fruits and vegetables in different regions (Gustavsson et al. ,2011, p.7)

5.2.1 Reasons for disposal

One reason for the enormous food waste conducted by households in industrialized countries is the fact that "people simply can afford to waste food". Retail store offer larger packages with discounts and offers like "getting one free", restaurants serve buffets at fixed prices or food manufactures produces ready to eat meals which are oversized. These are just some examples for the cause of food waste in industrialized countries (Stuart, 2009 cited by Gustavsson et al., 2011, p. 14). Another factor which plays an important role when considering the amount of waste of households is packing. 20-25% of food waste is caused by packaging. Williams et.al (2012) come to the conclusion that causes for food waste in the view of households are among others "too big packages" and "packages that are difficult to empty". The latter one is noted because households like packages which are "easy to empty, easy to reseal and easy to recycle" (Williams, Wikström, Otterbring, Löfgren, & Gustafsson, 2012, p. 19).

Additionally, the gender of the person in the household, who is mainly responsible for grocery shopping could be another factor of food disposal. When women are mainly responsible for the purchase of food, food waste is considerably higher (Koivupuro et al., 2012, p. 189).

Koivupuro et al. (2012) come to the conclusion that the number of occupants in one household, as the only socio-demographic factor, has a clear correlation with the amount of wasted food. The more persons live in one household, the more wasted food exist (Koivupuro et al., 2012, p. 188).

5.2.2 Ways to reduce waste

One method to prevent the amount of food waste is to strength public awareness. Williams et. al (2012) indicate that persons with environmental consciousness waste less food and pay more attention on packaging (Williams et al., 2012, p. 15). Political initiatives or education in schools regarding these topics are two options (Gustavsson et al., 2011, p. 14).

Keeping in mind that retailers offer larger packages with discounts, one way to reduce the amount of food waste, is to buy smaller packages and ignore advertorial offers.

Another way is to buy only the amount of food which will be ever eaten. This also includes offering smaller packages of food and eating a la carte in restaurants instead of buffets (Stuart, 2009 cited by Gustavsson et al., 2011, p. 14).

One opportunity to reduce waste at the producer level, is to sell these pieces of vegetables which have not the usual, normed form. An example of selling misshaped food instead of disposing it, happened in French. Being confronted with a huge amount of waste, Intermarché, a French supermarket chain, offered misshaped vegetable and fruits for a limited span of time. This misshaped fruit would have been disposed otherwise, because they were considered as "unfit for consumption"(Cliff, 2014). It is important that customer buy such unformed fruits. Indeed, this campaign was a huge success: Intermarché sold more than 1000 kg fruit per store in two days and enhanced its store traffic by 24%. (Russ, 2014, p. 10).

Figure 16 shows the campaign and two examples of misshaped fruits.

Figure 16 Campaign of Intermarché of mishaped fruits and vegetables (Cliff, 2014)

5.3 Waste of electrical and electronic equipment (WEEE)

As shown above, one aspect of washing is detergents. In this chapter, I would like to shift the focus on washing machines and how they affect pollution and environment. Washing machines are included in the term of WEEE. Jain & Garg (2011) define WEEE as "discarded products that have an electrical cable or battery" (p. 6). Khetriwal et al. (2009) include ten categories in which products are included by the term WEEE. These include among others large and small household appliances, equipment for telecommunications and IT, lighting as well consumer equipment and electrical and electronic tools (Khetriwal, Kraeuchi, & Widmer, 2009, p. 3)

7.3 million tons of waste electrical and electronic equipment (WEEE) were generated in Europe, 2002. The annual growth rate of WEEE is quantified with 3- 5 % (Abu Bakar & Rahimifard, 2008, p. 1). The growing amount of e-waste has significant social and economic impacts (Jain & Garg, 2011, p. 33). It is shown that the use of electric equipment and electronics such as washing machines has grown rapidly over the last twenty years. The technology age we live in and the pressure of producers to deliver the newest technology, (Khetriwal et al., 2009, p. 1) as well as the consumption rates (Jain & Garg, 2011, p. 3) lead to a quicker obsolescence of electronic equipment. As a result of this the volume of electronically waste grows rapidly (Khetriwal et al., 2009, p. 1). It is also believed that waste electric and electronic equipment (WEEE), is the fastest growing waste stream in Europe.

It is known that e-waste contain highly toxic substances which pose a threat for environment and health as well as for valuable raw materials (Khetriwal et al., 2009, p. 1). If the product lifespan of electronics of developed countries ends, most of them are shipped to India or other Asian countries. Cheap labor costs, as well as lack of working and environmental standards are some reasons for that unauthorized exports (Jain & Garg, 2011, p. 4). As we can see in Figure 17, it is an aim to close the loop of the material cycle of WEEE. The raw materials pass the stages of retailing and consumption and then being collected and recycled for the integration and production of new products and goods. Consumers return their old, broken among others direct to recycler or to designated collection points. From the latter, the WEEE is passed to disassemble establishments which manually dismantle the e-waste and decontaminate the waste by extracting the toxic elements in a protected and safe way. In the recycling centers, the e-waste is dismantled again and it will go through steps of shredding and sorting.

This process results in concentration of the main components like plastic, iron, glass, or aluminum. The rest of the waste, which does not include raw material is burnt. (Khetriwal et al., 2009, pp. 4–5).

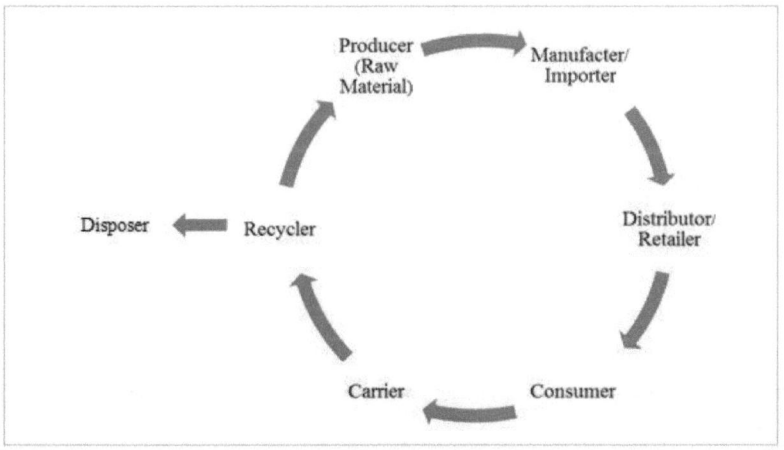

Figure 17 Loop of the material cycle of WEEE, (Khetriwal et al., 2009, pp. 4–5)

Recent trends in electric equipment and electronics (EEE) show the reduction of precious metal like palladium, silver or gold. These materials are included in EEE to reduce manufacturing costs
Recovering these metals is one of the main goals in the current EEE recycling practices. It is important to enhance the economic and environmental performance of WEEE recovery activities to build a long-lasting sustainability for the waste recovery industry (Abu Bakar & Rahimifard, 2008, p. 628).

5.3.1 Reasons for disposal

Customers often store their old, unused electronics several years before throwing it away.
Reasons for this behavior might be that customers are not aware of the opportunities of disposing e-waste i.e. where to dispose old electronics as well as the psychological factors (Kalana, 2010, pp. 137–138), this means that customer are also convinced that they old unused electronics contain material which can be recycled and has therefore some amount of value. This equipment could be sold to parties like e-waste contractors, assemblers or wastedealers. Instead of recycle the electronics, customers tend to wait for someone to buy the unused electronics from them (Kalana, 2010, p. 140).

Keeping this in mind, a huge amount of customers may be willing to give their electronic waste away, for free. Free Pickup services are also accepted as a method of giving away unwanted electronics (Kalana, 2010, p. 141).

Reasons why customers dispose are among others malfunction during use, lifespan elapsed and outdated. New products are cheap and high repair costs reflect the cost factors (Kalana, 2010, p. 139) .

5.3.2 Ways to reduce waste

We cannot deny the fact that the public awareness of disposing e-waste is still low comparing to other materials such as food. Customers store their unwanted electronics over years or even dispose e-waste with other waste (Kalana, 2010, p. 142).

Disposing materials which are classified as WEEE such as washing machines or TVs, lead to multi-material waste with materials like glass, plastic and metals. It is important to separate them from each other, if not this can be an enormous polluting effect on the environment. (Jain & Garg, 2011, p. 6)

The process of disposal can be divided in four categories: "repair, reduce, reuse and recycle" (Jain & Garg, 2011, p. 5). Repairing increases usability and the lifespan of an electronically product (Jain & Garg, 2011, p. 6). Reduce means separating materials which can harm the environment from the waste stream of WEEE before the final disposal. These toxic materials should be not mixed with the atmosphere and therefore disposed separately (Jain & Garg, 2011, p. 6). Another category is re-using. This means that customer re-use their repaired products again. This automatically save the costs of buying a new electronically product and it will automatically reduce the amount of e-waste. Re-using electric equipment and electronics (EEE) is an alternative which is beneficial for the environment and therefore also benefits the society (Jain & Garg, 2011, p. 6).The last category is recycling. This option is mostly used, in case reusing and repairing is not a suitable option. Household can send their used EEE, like washing machines for recycling. Some manufactures or companies like IBM or DELL accept old machines or EEE for recycling. Value materials are recovered and therefore reused. However, salvaging valuable materials also lead to high health and environmental costs (Jain & Garg, 2011, p. 6).

As we can see in the process of WEEE, it is crucial for households to be educated about this process and the importance of recycle e-waste in the correct way.

It is shown, that advertising can enhance the awareness of disposing electronically goods. It is a useful way of informing the consumers about the best method to manage the lifespan end of electronics (Kalana, 2010, p. 140). Besides advertising, the internet is an important factor in handling how to dispose WEEE. It could help to promote knowledge about e-waste and expand it globally.

These two types of communication and education are crucial in the world we live in. The media can influence the public's behavior in favor of how to handle with e- waste in the best and right way (Kalana, 2010, p. 140).

6 Limitations

One limitation of this thesis is the observation of three different areas. Of course a lot more areas can be identified like means of transport. Another aspect could be customers' impact on how renewable energy is used. The use of soolar panels on the roofs of the houses can be a start. This aspect was not part of this thesis.

We did not differentiate in different countries or regions. Socio-demographic aspects like age, gender or occupation were also not taken into account. This can be part of further research to gain more implications.

Another limitation is that this thesis is theoretically based, therefore no empirical analysis were made. To gain implications, empirical analysis are needed. Empirical analysis can include differentation in countries,

This thesis only represents the status quo of literature. The literature used was in English or German, other languages were not taken into account.

7 Implications and future research

Generally, it could be stated that reducing waste is much more than an economical issue. As we can see in this thesis, reducing waste affects nature in several ways. The outcome of this theses is to highlight different aspects of our daily life that contribute to economic growth but with the side effects of pollution.

We can see in this theses that education is needed for customers to realize what impact their behavior has in terms of sustainability and pollution. But not only education is needed among the global population. Angela Merkel, the chancellor of Germany, brings it to the point: what we also need is a paradigm shift:

> *"Worldwide we are still far away from a sustainable life, economy and work [...]; this has to be said quite openly. This fact is also reflected in huge economic and social disparaties. We are approaching the load limits of the earth, and they have already passed in part. We need a paradigm shift. If we fail such a paradigm shift, then we deprive future generations important means of livelihood."* (Angela Merkel, Speech on the 15th annual conference of the Council of Sustainable Development in Berlin 2015, own translation)

For this paradigm shift, it is crucial to raise awareness among people. This can be done by the producer side, for example by implementing marketing campaignes that draw attention to this issue.

Due to the fact that the relation of global economy and the global pollution issue was, is and will always be a sensitive topic of social responsibility, there might be some follow-up research topics to talk about. In order to investigate the global consumption of different branches, it would be interesting to oppose the consumer view to the producer view. Thus similarities or discrepancies, chances and risks could be revealed.

One other aspect could be to monitor campaigns that are already implemented in the market and to messure their influence on people, for example conducted by a survey.

As we can see, talking about economy and environmental pollution offers a controverse discussion among all stakeholders.

References

Abu Bakar, M. S., & Rahimifard, S. (2008). An integrated framework for planning of recycling activities in electrical and electronic sector. *International Journal of Computer Integrated Manufacturing*, 21(6), 617–630.

Aehle, W. (2007): Enzymes in Industry – Production and Applications.

Aldred J. (2008, February 28). Q&A Plastic bags. Rtrieved from http://www.theguardian.com/environment/2007/nov/13/plasticbags.pollution?gusrc=rss&feed=society, last checked 24.11.2015

Allwood, J.M., Laursen, S.E., Malvido de Rodriguez, C. & Bocken, N.M.P. (2006): Well Dressed? The Present and Future Sustainability of Clothing and Textiles in the United Kingdom. Cambridge.

Baier, A. & Frese, H. (2005): Vom Baumwollfeld bis in den Kleiderschrank. Hamburg. Online available under: http://www.pan-germany.org/download/fs_bw_b_schrank.pdf, last checked: 09.02.2016

Barilla Center for Food & Nutrition (2015): Double Pyramid 2015 - Recommendations for a sustainable diet. Online available under www.barillacfn.com, last checked 14.12.2015

Barry, A. (2006): A recipe for disaster – Will the Doha Round fail to deliver for development?: Oxfam Briefing Paper 87. Online available under: https://www.oxfam.de/system/files/20060427_arecipefordisaster_282kb.pdf. Last time checked: 19.02.2016

Bayerisches Landesamt für Umwelt (2013): Umweltwissen Praxis – Wasch und Reinigungsmittel. 1-15

Becker, J. (2012): Fair Trade and Corporate Social Responsibility. 12-21

Bianchi, C., & Birtwistle, G. (2010). Sell, give away, or donate: an exploratory study of fashion clothing disposal behaviour in two countries. *The International Review of Retail, Distribution and Consumer Research*, 20(3), 353–368.

Breyer, M. (2012). 25 shocking fashion industry statistics. Online available under http://www.treehugger.com/sustainable-fashion/25-shocking-fashion-industry-statistics.html, last checked 28.02.2016

Canavari, M.; Olson, K. D. (2007): Organic Food: Consumers' Choices and Farmers' Opportunities: Springer New York.

Christliche Initiative Romero (2012): WearFair - EIn Wegweiser durch den Label-Jungel bei Textilien. Berlin.

Claudio, L. (2007): Waste couture: environmental impact of the clothing industry, *Environmental Health Perspectives,* vol. 115, no. 9, pp. A448 - A454, online available under: http://www.ncbi.nlm.nih.gov/pmc/articles/PMC1964887/, last time checked: 01.03.2016

Cliff, M. (2014, July 16). Forget the ugli fruit, meet the ugly fruit bowl! French supermarket introduces lumpy and misshapen fruit and vegetables - sold at a 30% discount - to combat food waste.
Retrieved from http://www.dailymail.co.uk/femail/food/article-2693000/Forget-ugli-fruit-meet-ugly-fruit-bowl-French-supermarket-introduces-lumpy-misshapen-fruit-vegetables-sold-30-discount-combat-food-waste.html,last checked: 24.11.2015

Dahlgaard, J. & Dahlgaard, S. (2002). From defect reduction to reduction of waste and customer/stakeholder satisfaction (understanding the new TQM metrology). *Total Quality Management,* 13(8), 1069–1085.

Domina, T., & Koch, K. (1997). The Textile Waste Lifecycle. *Clothing and Textiles Research Journal,* 15(2), 96–102.

Domina, T., & Koch, K. (2002). Convenience and Frequency of Recycling: Implications for Including Textiles in Curbside Recycling Programs. *Environment and Behavior,* 34(2), 216–238.

eurostat FFS data (2015): Organic farming: number of farms, areas with different crops and heads of different types of animals by agricultural size of farm (UAA) and NUTS 2 regions. Online available under: http://appsso.eurostat.ec.europa.eu/nui/show.do, last checked: 23.10.2015.

Environmental Justice Foundation (2007): The Deadly Chemicals in Cotton. Online available under: http://www.pan-uk.org/attachments/125_the_deadly_chemicals_in_cotton_part1.pdf, last checked: 16.02.2016

Fair Wear Foundation (2009): Fair Wear Foundation: Labour Standards. Online available under: http://www.fairwear.org/488/labour-standards/. Last time checked: 17.02.2016

Frankfurter Allgemeine Zeitung (2014): Hausgeräte – von Siemens bleibt nur das Logo. Online available under: http://www.faz.net/aktuell/wirtschaft/hausgeraete-von-siemens-bleibt-nur-das-logo-13167421.html. Last time checked: 05.01.2016

Fletcher, K. (2008): Sustainable Fashion and Textiles. London: Earthscan.

Global Organic Textile Standard International Working Group (2014): Global Organic Textile Standard (GOTS) - Version 4.0. Online available under: http://www.global-standard.org/images/GOTS-version4-01Maerz2014_deutsch.pdf. Last time checked: 17.02.2016

Greenpeace (2012): Giftige Garne der große Textilien-Test von Greenpeace. Hamburg.

Gustavsson, J., Food and Agriculture Organization of the United Nations, & ASME/Pacific Rim Technical Conference and Exhibition on Integration and Packaging of MEMS, N. and Electronic Systems. (2011). Global food losses and food waste: extent, causes and prevention : study conducted for the International Congress "Save Food!" at Interpack 2011 Düsseldorf, Germany. Rome: Food and Agriculture Organization of the United Nations.

Haas, H. D., und H. M. Zademach (2005): Internationalisierung Im Textil- Und Bekleidungsgewerbe. Geographische Rundschau 57(2): 30–38.

Hallam D.: The organic market in OECD countries: past growth, current status and future potential, OECD Organic Agriculture: Sustainability, Markets and Policies, 179–186.

Henning, K. (2006): Wasch- und Reinigungsmittel – Inhaltsstoffe, Eigenschaften und Formulierungen.

ILO (2013): Bangladesh: Seeking better employment conditions for better socioeconomic outcomes. Geneva.

Institut Bauen und Umwelt e.V. (2016): Triangle of Sustainability. Online available under: http://construction environment.com/hp6259/Triangle of sustainability.htm. Last time checked: 03.03.2016.

Industrieverband Körperpflege- und Waschmittel e.V. (IKW): Bis zu 310 Euro jährlich sparen beim Waschen und Spülen. Online available under:

http://www.ikw.org/haushaltspflege/themen/wissenswertes/bis-zu-310-euro-jaehrlich-sparen-beim-waschen-und-spuelen. Last checked: 02.01.2016

Jackson, J. (2014, October 6). Assesing the Environmental Impact of the Fashion World. Online available under: http://www.environmentalleader.com/2014/10/06/assessing-the-environmental-impact-of-the-fashion-world/. Last checked: 28.02.2016

Jain, S., & Garg, K. M. (2011). Managing E-Waste in India: Adoption of Need Based Solutions. *Journal of Internet Banking & Commerce,* 16(3), 1–11.

Jenkin, M. (2015): 11 things we learned about achieving a zero-waste fashion industry, online available under: http://www.theguardian.com/sustainable-business/sustainable-fashion-blog/2015/jan/14/10-things-learned-zero-waste-fashion-industry, last time checked: 18.02.2016

Johnston, J. L.; Fanzo, J. C.; Cogill, B. (2014): Understanding Sustainable Diets: A Descriptive Analysis of the Determinants and Processes That Influence Diets and Their Impact on Health, Food Security, and Environmental Sustainability. *American Society for Nutrition, Advances in* Nutrition (4), 418–429.

Jung, S., & Jin, B. (2014). A theoretical investigation of slow fashion: sustainable future of the apparel industry: A theoretical investigation of slow fashion. *International Journal of Consumer Studies,* 38(5), 510–519.

Kalana, J. A. (2010). Electrical and Electronic Waste Management Practice by households in Shah Alam, Selangor, Malaysia. *International Journal of Environmental Sciences,* 1(2), 132–144.

Khetriwal, D. S., Kraeuchi, P., & Widmer, R. (2009). Producer responsibility for e-waste management: Key issues for consideration – Learning from the Swiss experience. *Journal of Environmental Management,* 90(1), 153–165.

Koch, K. & Domina, T. (1999). Consumer Textile Recycling as a Means of Solid Waste Reduction. *Family and Consumer Sciences Research Journal,* 28(1), 3–17.

Koivupuro, H.-K., Hartikainen, H., Silvennoinen, K., Katajajuuri, J.-M., Heikintalo, N., Reinikainen, A., & Jalkanen, L. (2012). Influence of socio-demographical, behavioural and attitudinal factors on the amount of avoidable food waste generated in Finnish households. *International Journal of Consumer Studies*, 36(2), 183–191.

Kristiansen, P.; Merfield, C. (2006): Overview of organic agriculture. In: Paul Kristiansen, Acram Taji und John Reganold: Organic agriculture. A global perspective. Collingwood, Vic.: CSIRO, 1–19.

Kristiansen, P.; Taji, A.; Reganold, J. (2006): Organic agriculture. A global perspective. Collingwood, Vic.: CSIRO.

Laitala, K. (2014). Consumers' clothing disposal behaviour - a synthesis of research results: Clothing disposal behaviour. *International Journal of Consumer Studies*, 38(5), 444–457.

Lexikon der Nachhaltigkeit (2014): „Lexikon der Nachhaltigkeit – Nachhaltigkeit in der Modebranche." Lexikon der Nachhaltigkeit. Online available under: http://www.nachhaltigkeit.info/artikel/nachhaltigkeit_in_der_modebranche_1764.htm. Last time checked: 17.02.2016

Luginbühl, C. & Musiolek, B. (2014): Im Stich Gelassen: Die Armutslöhne Der Arbeiterinnen in Kleiderfabriken in Osteuropa und Der Türkei. Online available under: http://lohnzumleben.de/im_stich_gelassen/, last time checked: 17.02.2016

McMullen, A. & Maher S. (2011): Let´s Clean Up Fashion – The state of pay behind the UK high street. Bristol. Online available under: http://www.women-ww.org/documents/LBL-LCUF2011.pdf. Last time checked: 19.02.2016

Morgan, L. R., & Birtwistle, G. (2009). An investigation of young fashion consumers' disposal habits. *International Journal of Consumer Studies*, 33(2), 190–198.

Muthu, S. S. (2015). Handbook of Sustainable Apparel Production. CRC Press New York.

Niinimäki, K. (2010). Eco-clothing, consumer identity and ideology. *Sustainable Development*, 18(3), 150–162.

OECD Studies on Environmental Policy and Household Behaviour Greening Household Behaviour Overview from the 2011 Survey - Revised edition: Overview from the 2011 Survey - Revised edition (2014): OECD Publishing.

Oxford University Press (2005): Oxford Advanced Learner´s Dictionary. Oxford New York

Pearson, D.; Henryks, J.; Jones, H. (2011): Organic food. What we know (and do not know) about consumers. *Renewable Agriculture and Food Systems* 26 (02), 171–177.

Pettinger, T. (31.Januar 20018). AD = C + I + G + X – M. from http://www.economicshelp.org/blog/245/readers-questions/ad-c-i-g-x-m/ , last checked : 07.March 2016

Publishing, OECD. (2013): OECD Studies on Environmental Policy and Household Behaviour. Overview from the 2011 Survey. Online available under: http://gbv.eblib.com/patron/FullRecord.aspx?p=1336565. Last checked: 11.12.105

Procter & Gamble (2014): Nachhaltigkeitsbericht 2014. Online available under: http://www.pg.com/de_DE/_pdf/PG_2014_Nachhaltigkeitsbericht.pdf Last checked: 15.01.2016

Ridoutt, B. G., Baird, D. L., Bastiaans, K., Darnell, R., Hendrie, G. A., Riley, M., Keating, B. A. (2014). Short communication: A food-systems approach to assessing dairy product waste. *Journal of Dairy Science*, 97(10), 6107 6110.

Ritch, E., Brennan, C., & MacLeod, C. (2009). Plastic bag politics: modifying consumer behaviour for sustainable development. *International Journal of Consumer Studies*, 33(2), 168–174.

Russ, M. (2014). When handed an ugly lemon. Marketing Magazine, 119(9), 10.

Schmitt, T. (2006): "Selbstmord-Serie: Tausend indische Bauern gehen in den Tod – SPIEGEL ONLINE." Spiegel Online, 12. November. Online available under: http://www.spiegel.de/wirtschaft/selbstmord-serie-tausend-indische-bauern-gehen-in-den-tod-a-446922.html. Last time checked: 18.02.2016

Schnepf, R.; Richardson, J. (2011): Consumers and Food Price Inflation: DIANE Publishing Company.

Starmanns, M. (2010): Corporate Responsibility in Der Modeindustrie. Geographische Rundschau 4:26–33.

Statista.com (2012): Statista Dossier – Haushaltsgeräte. 1-23

Statista.com (2015): Statista-Dossier zu Wasch-, Putz- und Reinigungsmitteln (WPR). 1-192

Statistische Ämter des Bundes und der Länder (2014): Gebiet und Bevölkerung. Online available under: http://www.statistik-portal.de/Statistik-Portal/de_jb01_jahrtab14.asp. Last time checked: 13.02.2016

Tukker A., Jansen B. (2006): Environmental Impacts of Products. *Journal of Industrial Ecology*, 10 (3), 159-182

Umweltbundesamt (2014): Gibt es umweltfreundliche Waschmittel?. Online available under: http://www.umweltbundesamt.de/themen/gibt-es-umweltfreundliche-waschmittel. Last time checked: 08.02.2016

Wagner, G. (2010): Waschmittel - Chemie, Umwelt, Nachhaltigkeit.

Williams, H., Wikström, F., Otterbring, T., Löfgren, M., & Gustafsson, A. (2012). Reasons for household food waste with special attention to packaging. Journal of Cleaner Production, 24, 141–148

Winter, C. K.; Davis, S. F. (2006): Organic Foods. In: *Journal of Food Science* 71 (9), 117-124.

Workshop on Organic Agriculture; OECD; OECD Workshop on Organic Agriculture (2003): Organic agriculture: sustainability, markets and policies. [OECD Workshop on Organic Agriculture, held on 23 - 26 September 2002 in Washington, DC]. Paris: OECD. Online available under http://www.sourceoecd.org/9264101500., last checked 14.12.2015

BEI GRIN MACHT SICH IHR WISSEN BEZAHLT

- Wir veröffentlichen Ihre Hausarbeit, Bachelor- und Masterarbeit
- Ihr eigenes eBook und Buch - weltweit in allen wichtigen Shops
- Verdienen Sie an jedem Verkauf

Jetzt bei www.GRIN.com hochladen und kostenlos publizieren